Something Borrowed

101 USEFUL TIPS FOR EVERY SAILOR

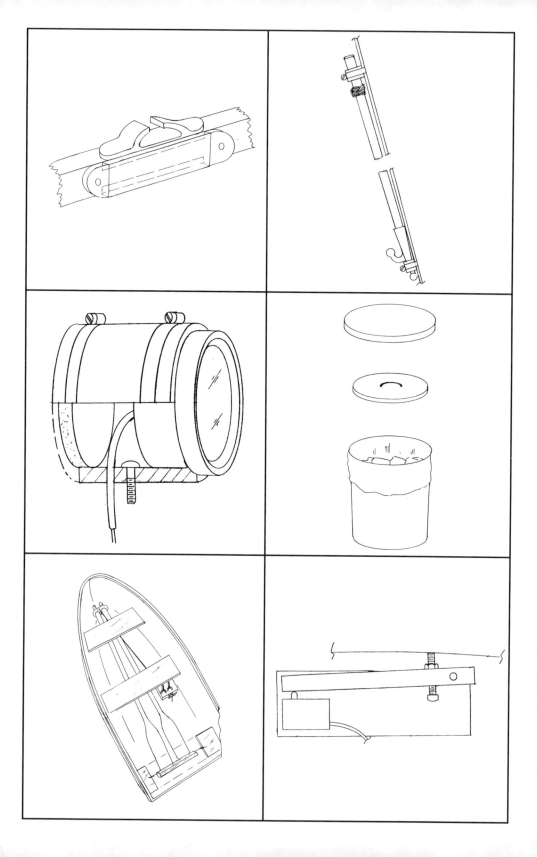

Something Borrowed

101 USEFUL TIPS
FOR EVERY SAILOR

JOEL W. GRAFFLEY

SHERIDAN HOUSE

To Al, who led the way aboard *Vintage*.

To Madaline, who sails with me aboard *Caper*.

To all of you, who follow us down the

sun-sparkled sea to paradise.

First published 1995 by
Sheridan House, Inc.
145 Palisade Street
Dobbs Ferry, NY 10522

Library of Congress Cataloging-in-Publication Data

Graffley, Joel W., 1931–
    Something borrowed : 101 useful tips for every sailor / Joel W. Graffley.
        p.   cm.
    ISBN 0-924486-93-7 (alk. paper)
    1. Boats and boating—Equipment and supplies.   I. Title.
    VW321.G69   1995
    623.8'6—dc20
                                                                95-25491
                                                                CIP

Design and Cover by Jeremiah B. Lighter

Printed in the United States of America

ISBN 0-924486-93-7

"Once you accept the fact that sailboats are to be worked upon, not sailed upon, your world becomes a whole lot simpler and happier."

ERIC TINNEY
Shared Pleasure

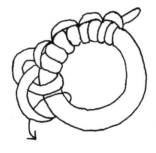

ACKNOWLEDGMENTS

No author can write a book without the assistance of others. It's especially true of *Something Borrowed* and me. I owe a word of thanks to so many people. Irwin Schmitt started me on this writing road. My wife, Madaline, is my proofreader and toughest critic. Bill Marsh allowed me the use of his computer for the final draft of the manuscript. Lothar Simon of Sheridan House liked what he saw. And many friends, acquaintances, and total strangers had their brains picked and ideas borrowed. My thanks to all of you.

Contents

Preface

I
On Deck
1

II
Below Deck
25

III

The Auxiliary
51

V
On the Hard
79

VI
Accessories
85

VII
Odds and Ends
99

Preface

Why borrow something? Each cruising boat is a unique blend of equipment, gear, and methods assembled for the safety and comfort of her crew. It is not the big items—electronics or fancy gadgetry—that make a vessel truly distinctive. Rather, it is those little techniques and innovations that are worth copying for your own use. *Caper*, our 35-foot yawl, is no exception. She is the culmination of many miles of cruising and more than a decade of living aboard. And since imitation is the truest form of flattery, I must admit that some of her "special features" have been freely borrowed from other craft.

Here is a collection of features and concepts that work well for Madaline and me. Wherever appropriate, I've credited the boat that was the source of the idea. Several items are, however, our own creation.

Feel free to help yourself to whatever seems like a good idea. Who knows, in time some other sailor may see it aboard your boat and adopt it for his or her very own.

On Deck

1
SAILING AIDS

2
GROUND TACKLE

3
DOCKING

4
INSTRUMENTS

5
IN THE COCKPIT

1 SAILING AIDS

Telltales

Caper's main mast is tall enough that Madaline and I find it uncomfortable to look to the top for a wind reference. We're not racing sailors, and we tend to steer by the feel of the wind on our faces. But now and again—especially in light air—it's nice to know where the wind is.

For this, we depend upon telltales. We manufacture our own from brightly colored spinnaker nylon. A lifetime supply is usually easy to scrounge from a sail loft. We cut the fabric into foot-long ribbons about 1/4-inch wide. Three telltales are taped to both port and starboard upper shrouds—one about waist high when I stand on deck, another 6 feet up, and the last as high as I can reach standing on the cabin top. Another is added to the backstay. Since *Caper* is a split rig, we frequently decorate her mizzen shrouds, too. This way, we can always quickly check the wind direction, even when we're below. The streamers don't foul themselves on the rigging wire, and they last one sailing season.

Friends have used old cassette tape for the same purpose, but we like the brighter colors of the nylon, and it seems to last longer.

Jacklines

When our Canadian friend Jim Hodges built his steel-hulled *Crocus*, he wanted a permanent system for a safety harness tether rather than rig jacklines when the wind honks up. His solution was to install genoa tracks instead of wooden eyebrows along the cabin sides, over the port lights. If Jim needs to go on deck in rough weather, he simply clips onto the car on the upwind side of the vessel and makes his way forward. The spring-loaded latch on the car locks into the track and limits the distance he can be thrown by a sea.

Resurfacing Decks

Caper, our yawl-rigged Pearson 35, was in her twenty-first year, and her decks were becoming slick from use. The molded-in texture was still there, but it served more to scatter reflected sunlight than provide a secure work platform.

Browsing through a sailing magazine, I came across an advertisement for a nonskid deck covering. Called TBS Viscom, it is a sheet polyurethane material marketed by Wichard Inc. of Simbury, Connecticut. The surface of TBS is a nonrepeating pattern of embedded microspheres that impart an extremely high coefficient of friction. The material is relatively thin—less than 1/8 inch in thickness—so it is easy to work with and adds little weight to the boat. It is available in sand, ivory and gray, and other colors on special order. We selected a light gray to approximate *Caper's* existing deck.

TBS is available in rolls 50 inches wide and 16 feet long. I knew that one roll would be inadequate to cover *Caper's* deck but could not readily determine if two would suffice. To solve this problem I made a scale drawing of the deck plan. I then sketched in a series of panels just a bit over 4 feet in length, about the width of the roll. Next, I laid out a pair of long, slender rectangles on the paper, simulating the two rolls of TBS and based on the same scale as the deck plan. I then reproduced each deck panel on one of the rolls, shifting them until I achieved the most economical orientation. In this way, I was able to determine that two

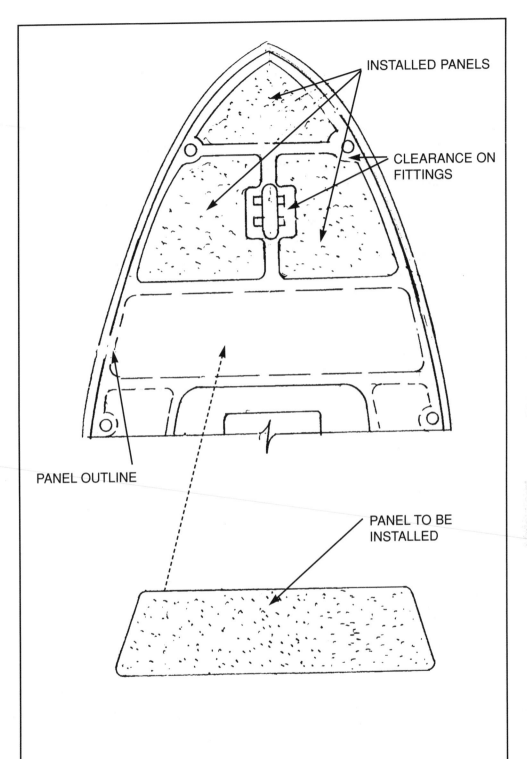

INSTALLED PANELS

CLEARANCE ON FITTINGS

PANEL OUTLINE

PANEL TO BE INSTALLED

Fig. 1.1: Slick decks can be resurfaced with nonskid panels cut
from full-size patterns.

rolls would be enough to resurface *Caper*'s decks and cockpit, with just a bit to spare for mats on the cabin top.

Madaline and I then busied ourselves making full-size patterns for each of the panels. We cut, fit, and taped posterboard for each piece that was to be cemented in place, no matter how small. Rather than attempt to fit each joint perfectly, we allowed for a gap of 1 inch between panels and along the toerails. We felt the gaps would also provide better drainage for water flowing across the decks. We found that the matching pieces on port and starboard were mirror images, and one pattern could be flip-flopped side to side.

We then unrolled the TBS upside down and laid out the patterns, also upside down, on the material, each in their specific position as determined by my scale drawings. Only a few adjustments were needed to provide the optimum use of the material. We then traced the outline of each pattern on the sheets with a felt-tip marker.

Finally, each pattern was set in its respective place on the boat and outlined with a soft pencil. This step gave us a final check for positioning the pieces of our jigsaw puzzle.

Starting at the bow, we worked aft, one panel at a time, cutting the TBS with a razor-blade knife. We rounded the corners to avoid the possibility of the material lifting after installation, cutting these radii with a large pair of scissors. After each panel was cut, it was dry fit into its appointed place for a final verification.

We then abraded *Caper*'s decks lightly with 60-grit sandpaper. This step was done primarily to clean the area of any dirt or oxidized finish. The old nonskid was not sufficiently coarse to warrant grinding or heavy sanding, and the few hairline cracks we noticed were not large enough to require special filling. After sanding the deck, we vacuumed it and then wiped it down with a clean rag soaked in acetone. I should note that the sanding operation was performed only where a panel was ready to be installed.

To install each panel, we applied a thin layer of epoxy to both the deck and the bottom surface of the material using the serrated edge of a regular linoleum trowel. (We purchased a gallon each of epoxy resin and hardener and found that amount adequate for the project.) After applying the cement, we carefully set the piece onto its designated place on the deck. We used a roller to force out the entrapped air and surplus epoxy and a putty knife to pick up excess cement. We feathered the edges with another rag soaked in acetone. We paid special attention to making cutouts around deck fittings, using scrap material to create patterns to ensure the best fit possible. To minimize the potential for accidentally shifting a newly laid panel before the epoxy "kicked," we installed the panels in a hop-scotch order.

After all the panels were secured, we took a small scrap of material to a local paint store. Starting with a white polyurethane enamel, the store clerk blended a color to match the TBS exactly. We painted between the panels to cover the remaining gelcoat and any visible epoxy. This was the final touch to a neatly executed project.

A shakedown sail was the real test. With *Caper's* low rail nearly awash, I was able to go surefootedly forward and work safely without difficulty. The nonskid covering provides a definite feeling of security when we hoist or furl the mainsail. In the cockpit, we find that we no longer tend to slide off the seats when we're sitting on the high side. The TBS is also comfortable to the rear end and can be sunbathed upon without leaving any trace of a pattern imprinted on the skin.

For anyone contemplating a similar project, I would offer this one bit of advice. If you want the job to go well, adhere to the carpenter's words of wisdom: "Measure twice, and cut once."

This material first appeared in *SAIL*, April 1991.

The On-deck Toolbox

In trying to be self-sufficient, we have loaded every tool that we can manage aboard our yawl. They are stowed in lockers, bilges, and under settees. Frequently, undertaking a quick job meant tearing apart Madaline's main cabin for just a few wrenches.

During a stint of work in a boatyard, I purchased a small plastic tackle box and filled it with spare tools that I needed on the job. When my hitch of work was over, I brought the box home and stowed it in the starboard lazarette. The next morning, I needed a screwdriver while my wife was baking; I grabbed the small box and simplified my life!

Here's an inventory of my on-deck toolbox:

> screwdriver with interchangeable blades
> adjustable wrench
> channel-lock pliers
> slip-jaw pliers
> vise-grip pliers
> electrical crimping tool
> wire brush
> broad knife scraper
> utility knife
> electrical tape

It's amazing to me just how much effort I've saved myself in no longer rooting through lockers and big tool boxes.

Perhaps I should not tout a product, but a number of years ago Madaline gave me a multipurpose tool called a Leatherman. In a belt sheath, it combines a knife, file, screwdrivers, punch, pliers, and ruler. It is guaranteed for twenty-five years. I use mine at least once every day.

Using the Marine Radio

Cruising with another boat can be a delightful experience. But at times it can also be frustrating. For instance, on a quiet morning in a peaceful anchorage you would like to talk to the other skipper to determine a departure time. But your friend's radio is off, your dinghy is lashed to the foredeck, and the distance between the two boats is too far to shout.

We experienced this situation while wandering with *Driftwood*. We resolved the communications dilemma by hoisting a pennant on a flag halyard. You often glance at the accompanying boat and soon spot the signal to turn on the VHF.

But use some judgment in the flag you select. It should not conflict with your surroundings. The Q flag is not appropriate in a port of entry, the dive flag is unacceptable in the Florida Keys, and flying one country's flag in another nation's waters could be seen as an insult. We hoist an obsolete yacht club burgee.

Safe Snoozing on Wheel Watch

While sailing in or near shipping lanes, it is wise to maintain a sharp lookout—at least one sweep of the horizon every 15 minutes—especially at night. That is the length of time that elapses from the moment a ship's range lights appear on the horizon until that vessel is upon you.

But if you are alone in the cockpit at night, it is easy to doze off. To assure that you will be awake for the next quarter-hour search, carry a kitchen timer in your slicker pocket. Twist the dial and relax: The alarm will remind or waken you.

2 GROUND TACKLE

Anchors

Anchors are much like the craft that they are intended to secure—each design is a compromise. The hook that sets well in sand, shell, or mud won't hold in coral or heavy grass. And since any cruising boat should be fitted with at least two anchors—do not carry twins—mix and match. *Caper*'s prime anchors are a plow and a fisherman. We also carry a Northill on the stern, a small lunch hook similar to a Danforth, and a monster fisherman storm anchor in the bilge.

Rodes

Bob Comstock aboard the Westsail 32 *Rhapsody* always claimed that chain was a sailor's best sleeping pill—you rest secure riding on chain. But Bob wasn't speaking of these 3-foot plastic-coated goodies sold in marine supply stores. They rust from within, and you won't even realize it. And they aren't nearly long enough. He was talking about heavy galvanized chain, with a minimum length equal to that of the vessel. *Caper* carries 100 feet of 3/8-inch proof coil chain on the plow and 50 feet on the fisherman. Of course, each is spliced onto a couple hundred feet of 3/4-inch nylon line. We seldom drag, and the motion at anchor is much easier than it would be if we were riding on only a nylon rode.

Obviously, even galvanized chain rusts eventually, but the rust is very visible. New chain is expensive (at least for a cruising couple on a retirement income). As an alternative, I periodically inspect and recondition our chain inventory. If the chain is badly rusted, I drag it behind our van for a few miles down an unpaved road. Dirt, sand, and gravel do an excellent job of abrading away nearly all the oxidation. Then I paint the chain with a generous coating of Pettit Trailer-Coat. This zinc-rich finish is extremely tenacious and is a fair substitute for a fresh application of hot-dip galvanize. I remove any severely corroded links and replace them with shackles.

Installing a swivel shackle part way down the chain allows you to attach a second anchor and rode. This arrangement is ideal for setting a Bahamian moor in an area of reversing tidal flow. Two rodes over the bow will intertwine, but a single rode down to a swivel allows the boat to swing freely on the tide.

Rode Riders

Before we set out cruising, I took the advice of an old salt, Eric Cheatley of the knockabout yawl *Wee Lass*. I purchased a 10-pound sounding lead. It not only augments the depthsounder, but can be used as a sentinel, or rode rider, to increase the catenary of the anchor line in a blow. And we have used it for this purpose. Thank you, Eric.

Avoiding Keel Tangle

Look around your anchorage and you will see that some boats dance more on their anchor than others. The dancers are craft with fin keels. This motion is the downside of their quick response to the helm, while their long-keeled sisters lie more docilely to the wind.

Often, this dancing whipsaw motion—especially in tidal flow—leads to the nylon rode becoming wound around the keel or rudder. This situation is definitely not

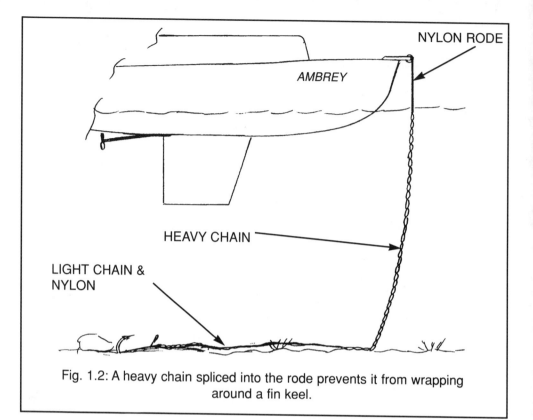

NYLON RODE

AMBREY

HEAVY CHAIN

LIGHT CHAIN &
NYLON

Fig. 1.2: A heavy chain spliced into the rode prevents it from wrapping around a fin keel.

fun and sometimes requires you to dive under the boat to free the line.

Ambrey carried 30 feet of 5/16-inch chain above the anchor, shackled in turn to a nylon rode. She did the anchor dance and twice fouled the line on her keel. Her skipper, Fred Neal, solved this problem by cutting the rode at 50 feet and splicing in 20 feet of 1/2-inch chain. He would pay out the ground tackle until the heavy chain just cleared the bow roller. By its own weight, the chain hung straight down when the air was light, keeping the nylon line well below the keel. The boat was now free to move with tide or wind without fouling her keel or rudder. In strong winds, the ground tackle grew taut and the extra chain provided a deeper catenary, keeping the anchor secure in the bottom.

Cheek Plates

Our yawl's toerails are teak. The anchor chain and nylon rodes scratched the varnish and sometimes even abraded the wood itself where they passed through the chocks and led down to the water. To counteract this problem, we installed cheek plates on the outside of the toerails. Two pieces of 1/2-inch-thick teak were ripped to match the height of the rails, and the ends were rounded. Twenty-gauge stainless steel was then tightly formed around each slat. The assemblies were screwed to the outside of the toerails, centered beneath the chocks. The screw holes were plugged.

Now the stainless steel guards absorb all the abuse. *Caper*'s teak remains pristine, even during lengthy cruises. And the stainless steel can be readily replaced when it is worn.

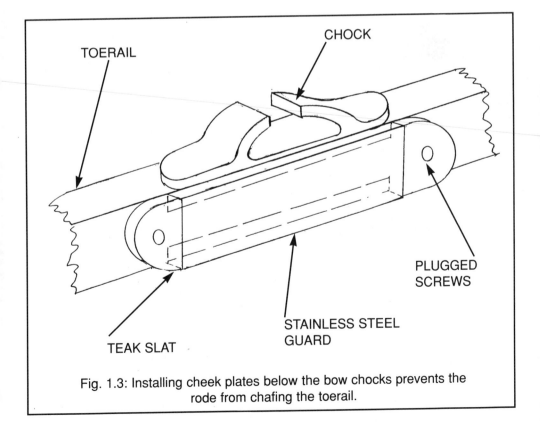

Fig. 1.3: Installing cheek plates below the bow chocks prevents the rode from chafing the toerail.

3 DOCKING

Jumper Lines

Approaching a strange dock is always a bit intimidating, and you simply cannot stop a boat with a bow line. Madaline and I sail by ourselves, and I frequently singlehand, so we need a foolproof method for docking. Our solution is a "jumper line," a heavy line always made fast to the base of the mast. As *Caper* comes alongside, my wife merely steps onto the dock and snubs the jumper line around a cleat or piling. This action takes the way off the vessel and swings her gently against the dock.

Boat Hooks

Real boat hooks, those with a long wooden handle, are hard to find these days. But you can make one yourself. Use a long shovel handle, closet pole, or flag staff. Most chandlers or mail-order houses still carry bronze or galvanized boat-hook tips. Taper one end of the wood pole to match the bore of the tip. Rivet the tip in place by running brass rod through the holes precast in the tip and peen the ends. A Turk's head rove around the base of the handle prevents the boat hook from slipping through your hands.

"But," you say, "that long boat hook won't fit in my lazarette." Right, but two plastic pipe couplings secured to a shroud make a perfect mounting bracket, and you won't have to scramble to locate the boat hook when you need it. The lower coupling should be only large enough to seat the tip of the hook, while the upper one must easily receive the handle. Using stainless steel hose clamps, install them on the shroud about 1 foot closer together than the overall

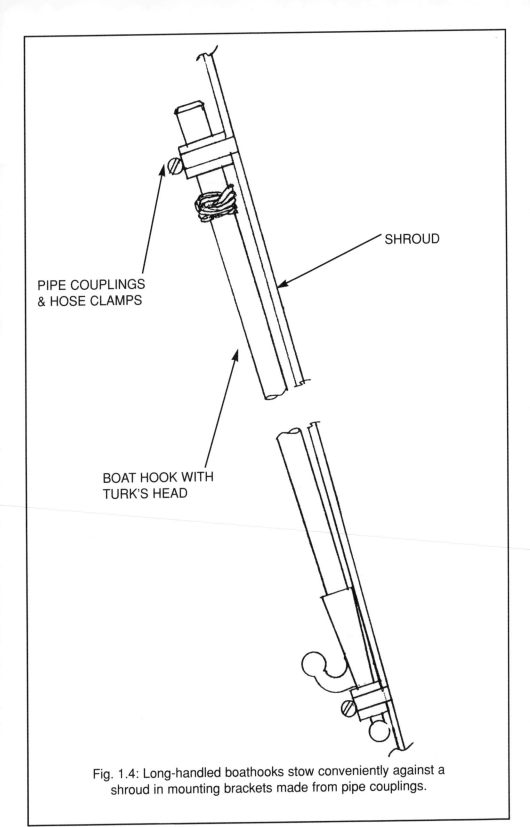

SHROUD

PIPE COUPLINGS
& HOSE CLAMPS

BOAT HOOK WITH
TURK'S HEAD

Fig. 1.4: Long-handled boathooks stow conveniently against a
shroud in mounting brackets made from pipe couplings.

length of the boat hook. With the tip downward, slide the boat hook up into the top coupling and then lower it into the bottom one. Even in the roughest weather, our boat hooks stay firmly in place with this design.

Canal Fenders

When Madaline and I lived in the north, we sailed the sweetwater seas—the Great Lakes. We often reached our cruising grounds via the region's many canal systems, such as Canada's Trent-Severn Waterway and New York's Erie Canal and its subsidiaries.

All these canals are built over rugged terrain and require a series of locks. The lock walls are typically concrete and are jagged and scarred from years of service. We did not feel comfortable subjecting *Caper*'s inflatable plastic fenders to such hard use, knowing their life span would be greatly shortened. Most canal authorities ban the use of old tires—if they become lost they can be a hazard to other craft, and they visually trash the waterways. Hay bales are sometimes used, but they are fragile and disintegrate too easily.

Our solution was to craft fender boards. We cut wooden four-by-fours into pieces about 2 feet long. We beveled both ends of each piece at 45 degrees on a common surface and padded the surface opposite the bevel with fire hose. Finally, we drilled a hole through one end and passed a line through it. The line suspends the fender from a stanchion and cleat. The fender hangs vertically, with the padded side against the hull. The beveled side faces out, permitting the fender to ride easily up and down the jagged lock walls much like a sled would. We used six fenders on each side of *Caper*, and she never received a scratch.

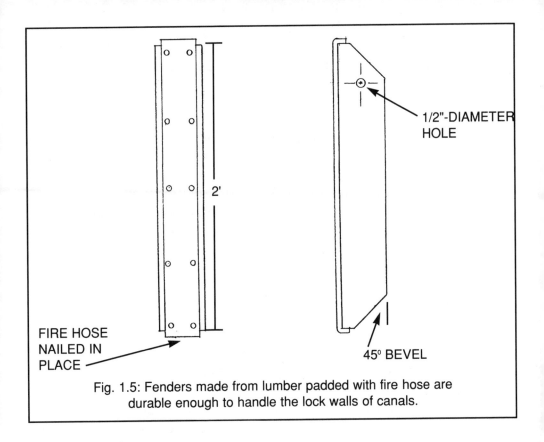

FIRE HOSE NAILED IN PLACE

2'

1/2"-DIAMETER HOLE

45° BEVEL

Fig. 1.5: Fenders made from lumber padded with fire hose are durable enough to handle the lock walls of canals.

Patching Inflatable Fenders

During a cruise to the Bahamas, one of *Caper*'s large inflatable fenders was punctured by a piece of steel projecting from a dock. I first tried to patch the hole by inserting a glue-impregnated string, similar to patching a tubeless tire. No luck. After returning to the States, I purchased an aerosol can of tire sealant. Still no luck. At long last, I poked a small amount of 3M 5200 sealant into the hole with a toothpick. I removed the toothpick and allowed the sealant to set for 24 hours. My fix is still holding the first fill of air.

This trick has also proven to be a successful means of patching inflatable boats.

Backing under Power

All single-screw boats back to port or starboard because of the direction of the propeller rotation and thrust. To back straight, use the engine only to get sternway onto the vessel; then shift into neutral. Without the rotational effect of the screw, the rudder will control the boat. As she slows, use another brief application of power to maintain momentum.

4 INSTRUMENTS

The Forward-Looking Depthsounder

Once I remarked to my late friend Al Bernreuther of *Vintage* that I would love to have a forward-looking depthsounder or similar device that could read the water depth off *Caper's* bow as we crept into a new anchorage. Al looked smug and told me his method.

"Rig a heavy sinker on the end of a spin-casting line and a very light bobber about a foot farther up the line than your boat's draft. If she draws four feet, put the bobber at five feet. Cast the line ahead of you. If the bobber sinks, your channel has enough depth in that area. If it floats, the line to the sinker is slack and you're heading for the shallows."

Instrument Mounting

When we installed a tachometer, I was not about to bore a large hole in *Caper's* cockpit. A visit to a local hardware store provided a solution, however. I purchased a rubber

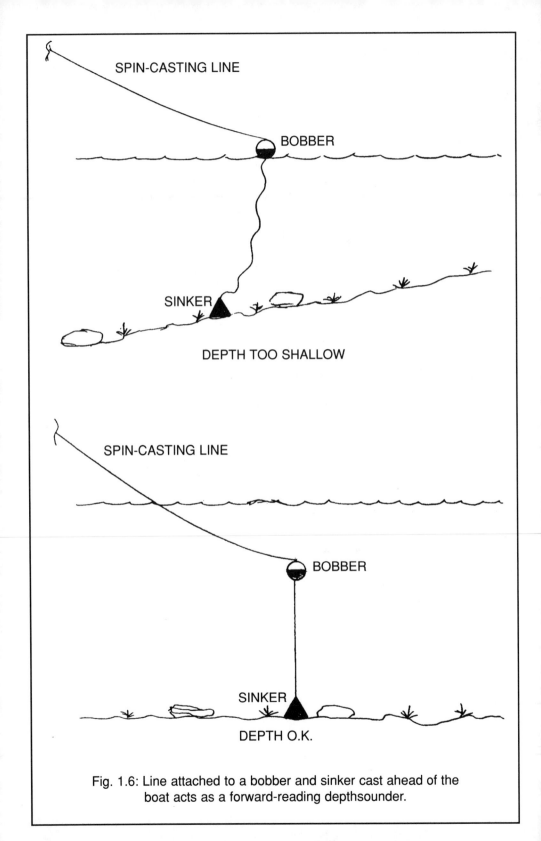

SPIN-CASTING LINE

BOBBER

SINKER

DEPTH TOO SHALLOW

SPIN-CASTING LINE

BOBBER

SINKER

DEPTH O.K.

Fig. 1.6: Line attached to a bobber and sinker cast ahead of the
boat acts as a forward-reading depthsounder.

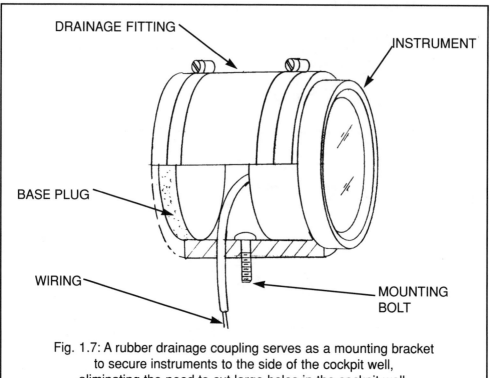

DRAINAGE FITTING

INSTRUMENT

BASE PLUG

WIRING

MOUNTING BOLT

Fig. 1.7: A rubber drainage coupling serves as a mounting bracket
to secure instruments to the side of the cockpit well,
eliminating the need to cut large holes in the cockpit wall.

drain coupling that fit snugly over the tach. The instrument was secured at one end of the coupling by hose clamps, and a wooden disc slipped into the other end was similarly held in place as a watertight seal. Two holes drilled in the side of the coupling provided for a mounting screw and an exit for the wiring. When I secured the assembly to the side of the cockpit well, I sealed both coupling and fiberglass with silicone rubber to exclude any water.

This material first appeared in *Motor Boating & Yachting*'s "Boatkeeper."

5 IN THE COCKPIT

Cockpit Grating

Our shakedown prior to becoming liveaboards was a six-week cruise from Lake Ontario to Georgian Bay in Lake Huron and return. We found that even in those northern latitudes, *Caper*'s cockpit sole became so hot on summer days that we burned our bare feet and we had to stand on wet towels. I resolved to correct that situation the following winter.

Rather than build an all-teak grating, which would have been very costly, we elected to go with the then-new plastic interlocking tiles. But *Caper*'s cockpit is not a true rectangle, and the binnacle, mizzenmast, and fuel fill are

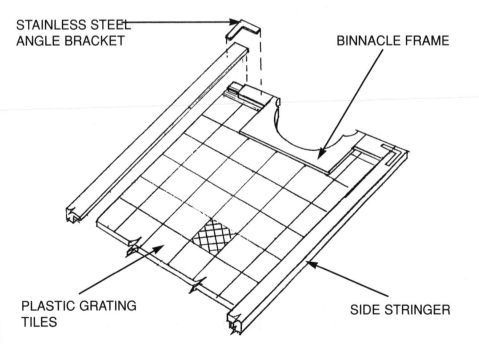

STAINLESS STEEL
ANGLE BRACKET

BINNACLE FRAME

PLASTIC GRATING
TILES

SIDE STRINGER

Fig. 1.8: Plastic tiles set in a teak frame provide an alternative to a
costly all-teak cockpit grating.

all mounted on the cockpit sole. Therefore, a neat trimming job was out of the question. So out came the joinery tools. I ripped 1-inch teak into boards 3 inches wide. One edge was routed out 3/4 inch square, and the others were rounded to break the sharp edge. Using these boards, I built frames to fit around the binnacle and mizzen bases. The top ends of these were rabbeted. Long port and starboard side stringers were rabbeted beneath to match. On all of these parts, the lower routed edge faced into the cockpit well, providing a recess to receive the outer edge of the cut-to-size plastic grating.

The frames were screwed together using stainless steel angle braces, and the assembled plastic grating was trimmed to fit the recess. I bored a 3 1/2-inch hole in the grating with a hole saw over the fuel fill. Then I turned a shouldered wooden cap to act as a cover.

After everything was dry fitted, the various wooden parts were disassembled. Madaline applied several coats of polyurethane varnish to each. She finds this finish to be superior in high-traffic areas.

Our cockpit grating is now more than twelve years old. The only maintenance is an annual application of a few coats of polyurethane to the wood and an occasional washdown to the plastic and the cockpit sole. The plastic is molded with a nonskid surface on the top. Integral feet raise it off the sole, so that air circulates and water drains readily.

Now we sail barefoot once again.

The Gimbaled Cockpit Table

Caper has a large cockpit, and her wheel is set close to the bridgedeck. This configuration is great for sheltering the helmsman behind the dodger and for seating several guests. But there is no place to mount a cockpit table. We

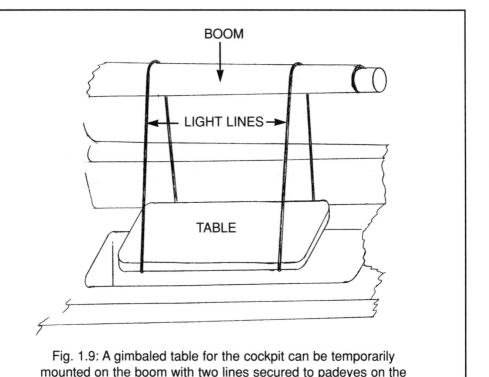

BOOM

← LIGHT LINES →

TABLE

Fig. 1.9: A gimbaled table for the cockpit can be temporarily mounted on the boom with two lines secured to padeyes on the underside of the table.

happily borrowed this solution from Ruth Comstock aboard *Rhapsody*.

Our cockpit table is long enough to seat two people along each side, and it stows in a lazarette. A padeye is screwed to the bottom of the table at each of the four corners. Two lightweight nylon lines with stainless steel S-hooks are tied to the padeyes on one side of the table. The lines are passed over the main boom, and the hooks are slipped into the padeyes on the opposite side. Immediately, we have a free swinging, gimbaled cockpit table for our sundown parties.

Lazarette Latches

Mike Jackman tells a humorous story that could well have led to tragedy. The shaft packing was dripping too much aboard *Ya Ha* while she was anchored in Boot Key Harbor in the Florida Keys. Wrenches in hand, Mike climbed into the lazarette to tighten the packing. While he was down in the bilge, a fishing boat went by, throwing a substantial wake. The boat rocked, and the cockpit seat/lazarette cover slammed shut, normally an event of no consequence. But in this instance, the hasp of the latch was above the staple. It swung down over the staple, locking the cover with Mike inside! And there he stayed for a couple of hours until a fellow sailor in a passing dinghy heard his cries for help.

Had Mike been working in a deserted anchorage, rather than one of the busiest, he could well have perished.

What is the arrangement on your boat? Do the lazarette latches engage on contact?

Below Deck

1 CABIN COMFORT

Sailors are a masochistic breed. We fully expect to be hot, cold, or wet while indulging in our favorite sport. Besides, a bit of agony adds spice to the sea story about our most recent cruise. But this tolerance ceases when the anchor is down and we go below. After all, we reason, a snug cabin should be our personal harbor of refuge from the whims of a not-always-congenial Mother Nature. Although the cabin may be a small shelter from the elements, a variety of improvements can raise the level of comfort on an overnight trip, on a long cruise, and especially when living aboard.

Insulation

You will achieve a great deal of comfort by the purely passive means of insulating the inside of the hull and underside of the decks. Cork tile can be used effectively on exposed surfaces. Polyurethane insulating board can be used inside lockers and beneath the decks. Stay away from Styrofoam—it can burn, and when it is wet, it loses its insulating ability.

Insulation provides three major benefits. It naturally minimizes temperature fluctuations down below. Along with proper ventilation, it keeps your cabin from becoming one huge culture dish for growing mildew. Finally, it tends to soundproof your boat, and the wind won't be nearly so demoralizing when you're snugged down in that big cozy bunk.

Heat from Lamps and Stoves

You're bound to wonder what a southern liveaboard knows about keeping warm. The answer is, in reality, quite a lot. Occasionally along Florida's coasts the dockside water supply lines freeze. Temperatures in the forties (Fahrenheit) are not uncommon.

Sure, you can huddle below, all bundled up, but that's not necessary. In moderately cool damp weather, gimbaled oil lamps are a godsend. We have three onboard—one each in the galley, main saloon, and forward cabin. They do a very adequate job of raising the cabin temperature. This is especially true if you heed my earlier preaching about insulation.

Caper is a greedy mistress, so we constantly shower her with gifts. One winter, we installed a hanging version of the Aladdin mantle lamp. These lamps are usually table models but are modified to hanging or gimbaled styles by Faire Harbor of Scituate, Massachusetts. They are also available from Aladdin Industries, Inc., in Nashville, Tennessee. On a chilly evening, we can laze in 75 degrees of warmth and even read by the bright white light the mantle gives off. There is no hiss as there is from pressurized mantle lanterns.

We burn mineral spirits in both the Aladdin lamp and the smaller oil lamps. We find that this fuel is less expensive, more readily available, and burns cleaner with less odor than kerosene. (Incidentally, one fellow we know uses jet fuel as a substitute in his kerosene cooking stove.)

There is one drawback to heating by oil lamps. Water is a byproduct of combustion, and the lamps vent inside. Therefore, although the warmer cabin air can aborb more moisture, there is still a slight increase in relative humidity.

For truly cold weather, you simply cannot beat the toasty warmth of a wood-burning stove or fireplace. These sources of heat vent to the outside and dry the cabin wonderfully. We were fortunate indeed that Bob Chapman,

Caper's original owner, saw fit to install a small wood-burning stove. Each autumn down here in the Keys, I lay in our winter fuel supply—an 8-foot two-by-four, cut into 6-inch lengths and split, backed up by a bag of charcoal. By comparison, we burned that much on a weekend on the Great Lakes. Friends have a diesel stove aboard their Morgan Out Island 41—it will drive you out of the cabin with its warmth!

One last word of caution. *Any* device that heats through the combustion of fossil fuel produces deadly carbon monoxide gas. Therefore, always leave a port light and/or hatch partially open to allow a fresh supply of air into the cabin when you use any of these heat sources.

Cold Days, Bright Cabins

On those chilly days when the north winds prowl your home waters, it's nice to curl up with a book and laze the hours away. It can be even more pleasant if the cabin is bright and cheerful. As part of our insulating program, *Caper's* hatch covers were fitted with Acrilan hoods over foam to minimize the effects of solar radiation. Solar film was installed on her port lights for the same reason. The results were gratifying, except that the cabin was a tad gloomy on those rare dark days.

We had already fastened Velcro tape around the fore and main hatches for insect screens. I purchased some clear vinyl sheeting used for dodger windows, cut pieces to match the screen size, and stitched the locking Velcro material to them. Our hatches can now be open, allowing light to enter, even during sieges of cold weather.

Caper's companionway doors are each fitted with a small window. But on really gloomy days, we open the doors and place two transparent plastic slides into the track where the dropboards fit. The slides are built from 1/4-inch-thick polycarbonate, with pine on the sides and

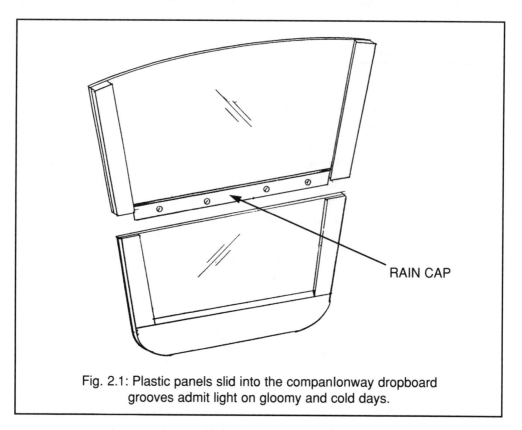

RAIN CAP

Fig. 2.1: Plastic panels slid into the companionway dropboard grooves admit light on gloomy and cold days.

the bottom of the lower piece to fit firmly in the dropboard grooves. A beveled strip screwed on the outside of the bottom edge of the upper panel provides a rain-tight overlap. On extremely cold nights, we insert the plastic panels and close the companionway doors over them to further minimize heat loss.

Keeping Your Cool

All the preceding insulating projects have the dual purpose of keeping the boat warm in winter and cool during the hot summer season. Of course, in the subtropics and tropics these passive cooling measures are not enough. Our prime source of dockside summertime comfort is an RV-type air conditioner secured to the main cabin hatch.

In addition, we have found that awnings make a

tremendous difference in minimizing the heat load on a boat and, in turn, the strain on the air-conditioning unit. A canopy of white fabric such as Acrilan provides shelter from the sun and the rain. It does not, however, allow any convective cooling, since the heat radiated from the boat is trapped beneath the cover. However the open-weave material used by growers to shade their crops from the hot sun makes an excellent awning. This material acts like the leaves of a tree—it refracts the sunlight, dissipating the heat, and allows the shaded area to ventilate. Unfortunately, it does not offer shelter from the rain. The material can also be hung from a regular awning as a side or stern fly.

Awnings in the Wind

We have known Don Crombie of *Driftwood* for many years now. He claims that he's not a sailor, merely a guy who travels on a sailboat. But he has sailed for many a mile.

I visited Don and Helen one breezy springtime morning. The cockpit awnings on nearby boats were flapping wildly, but not theirs. Glancing up, I wondered out loud, "Why?"

"Oh," replied Don, "I keep some old three-quarter-inch line handy, and when the wind cranks up, I just lay the line on top of the awning. The distributed weight holds it down."

Of Bugs, Critters, and Such

By now, every cruiser must know that Avon's Skin-So-Soft is one of the best insect repellents around. It makes you smell good too.

Boric acid is death on roaches if you sprinkle it where they are likely to travel. But if you are boarded by Coast

Guard or customs officials, be prepared to explain what that white powder really is.

Not long ago, Sara Marsh of *Pendragon* told us that bay leaves discourage spiders: "Use bay leaves to keep spiders at bay." Her pun, not mine.

Cruising up Florida's west coast, we sometimes spend a night anchored in Little Shark River, deep in the Everglades. We always anticipate insects there after sundown. But one night we were plagued with no-see-ums from dusk until dawn. They are tiny enough to come through our screens, and their bite is like fire. The onslaught was so bad that we debated making a straight shot from Marco Island to the Keys on our return, rather than wend our customary easy-going way back home. But farther up the coast, Debbie Bump of *Mary Ellen Carter* (one of *Caper*'s sloop-rigged sisterships) gave Madaline a bottle of Screen Pruf, and our world was good again. At anchor back in Little Shark River, Madaline wet a cotton swab with the fluid and coated the port light, companionway, and hatch screens. We slept peacefully and in comfort. The next morning, the folks on a boat near us reported that they had closed and dogged everything at sunset just to survive.

Rats !

Loren Butman and Retta Jaymes raised cattle in Oregon during the summer and sailed the Keys and Bahamas in the winter. One autumn, they returned to their boat to find it devastated by unwelcome guests—rats.

The boat had been wet-stored in a marina upon their return from an island cruise. Loren and Retta assumed that the rodents entered the otherwise sealed vessel through the bilge blower vents. She was diesel powered and no hoses were ever connected to the vents. The rats fell into the bilge and were trapped within the boat. They did enormous damage until they finally died of thirst.

When we learned of the problem, Jack Reck, Dayton Lovelein, and I discussed the matter, seeking an ounce of prevention. *Manx* and *High Roller* are wet-stored in our basin each summer for six months. We leave *Caper* for as long as three months. And we knew we could easily encounter rodents in another marina while cruising.

Our solution was simple and inexpensive. Each of us purchased packets of bronze wool scouring pads. We packed several pads into each vent. Air still circulates, but rats aren't likely to chew their way through the mesh.

2 THE MAIN CABIN

The Perfectly Fit Carpet

When Madaline decided to lay down carpeting on *Caper's* cabin sole, we were at a loss how to install it properly. Bob Wheatley of *Equinox* guided us in making an absolutely perfect template that could be laid on the carpet and outlined, so the carpeting could be cut to the exact size. I have since used this technique in cabinet making and other projects where a precise fit is required.

Start with several sheets of posterboard. Spread them on the cabin sole, slightly overlapping, and secure all the joints with masking tape. Cut smaller pieces to fill in the gaps between the full sheets and bulkheads, settee fronts, and so on. Continue cutting and taping progressively smaller pieces until every gap has been closed. Carefully remove the template to the dock or some other flat area, and lay it upside down. Tape all the seams on the face now exposed. When the taping is completed, you have an exact and strong replica of the surface you want to cover.

Lay out the carpet, upside down. Place the template over it, also upside down. Trace the template's outline on the carpet backing with a felt tip marker. Remove the template. Cut the carpet with a utility knife along the marked outline. Roll the carpet, and carry it below. Unroll it into the desired place.

If the template was made properly, you have a truly professional installation with only a minimum of final trimming.

Compact Cabin Tables

Sailboat designers and builders just can't seem to grasp the concept that couples sail and cruise. There is simply no great need for multi-bedrooms and banquet tables on board. Do you know five or six other people with whom you'd want to share a cruise?

Long-time liveaboards Fred and Maxine Neal of the sloop *Ambrey* have fitted their boat with a wonderfully comfortable cabin and a saloon table worthy of Thomas Jefferson's ingenuity. It is a traditional dropleaf table, except that the center leaf is only about 2 inches wide. When the table is in use, its forward end rests on a support attached to the mast. The after end rides on bearings over a vertical stainless steel tube that is fastened to the forward face of the galley's peninsula sink cabinet. To store the table, Maxine simply drops the leaves and lifts the table up on the tube. The table is then swung 90 degrees so that it nests on a small ledge along the sink cabinet at the end of the settee.

Shortly after Madaline saw *Ambrey*'s table, she announced that *Caper*'s cabin was too small. I eventually determined that it was time for me to build a new cabin table that

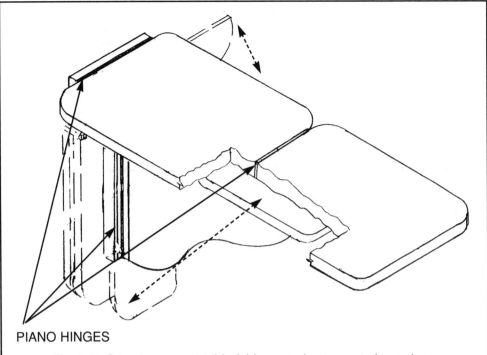

PIANO HINGES

Fig. 2.2: *Caper's* compact table folds up and out; a gate leg swings
in to brace the wooden tongue that supports the hinged joint.

would take less space. My final design was a double-leaf af-
fair that folds up and out from our peninsula refrigerator
box. A wooden tongue projects from beneath the outer leaf
to support the hinged joint between the two leaves when the
table is open. A gate leg swings out from its nesting position
along the box surface and braces the tongue. When the table
is folded away, a web strap with a snap holds the leaves together at the top. Our table raises and lowers in seconds and
accommodates four. And when dinner is over, the settee is
available for unimpeded lounging.

Odor Absorber

Carol Martin has a unique means of controlling odors
aboard *Crocus*, especially when the boat is to be laid up or
left closed for a while. She places a few clothes drier anti-

static sheets around the cabin. They absorb odors and freshen the air.

3 THE GALLEY

Nonskid Dishes

Not long ago, Bob Trudell of *Waymar* reminded me of an old trick. A circular bead of silicone rubber applied to the bottom of any plate or bowl makes it nonskid. There's no need to buy expensive dishes from your local marine dealer. Simply turn the plate over, and apply the silicone rubber. Then set the plate right side up on a flat surface covered with wax paper. Press down gently to flatten the bead of silicone. Allow it to cure for a few hours. Peel off the wax paper, and your dinner will slide off the plate before the plate slips in heavy seas.

A Knife Holder

David Crane of the ketch *Sea Wind* is a fine craftsman with wood and an equally fine friend. Several years back, he made Madaline a knife holder. It consists of layers of teak with slots routed into them to accept the blades. The block is slightly narrower than our companionway ladder, where he mounted it. Our frequently used knives are always within hand's reach in the galley.

LPG Leak Test

When we first moved aboard, many years ago, we converted the alcohol stove to kerosene. After a long relationship with fouled burners, leaks, and flare-ups, we installed a whole new propane system. We love the convenience of gas. But because of this fuel's explosive potential, we have developed a monthly leak-test routine.

With one burner open and operating, we close the valve to the burner, extinguishing the flame. The solenoid at the fuel tank is now de-energized. This isolates the fuel in the gas supply line, but it is under a static pressure of only about 1 psi. After an hour, with the solenoid still turned off, we open the burner and ignite it. If the flame burns well for a few seconds before going out, there is no leak—there is gas still in the line. But if the burner does not ignite, the gas has leaked. And we have serious trouble!

Sounding the Propane Tank

When Al Bernreuther sailed with me for the last time, *Caper* had her new propane stove. Al was a sea cook and loved the instant heat, but he fretted about running out of fuel. One evening, we sat and brainstormed the problem instead of cheating each other at cards.

We finally recalled that liquid petroleum gas (LPG or propane) is actually stored as a liquid. From our long-ago thermodynamics courses, we deduced that heat is required to flash the liquid to a gas if no change in pressure takes place. And since the heat is needed at the surface of the liquid, heat will be drawn from the surrounding areas.

With our newly found knowledge, we poured hot water over the tank. Voilà! The tank became warm except in one place—at the surface of the liquid, where it was absorbing heat to flash to vapor. There the tank was cool, and we knew how much fuel it still held.

Try it; it works!

Lining the Reefer Box

In my, of course totally unbiased, opinion, the insulation provided in the iceboxes of nearly all production sailboats is essentially nonexistent.

When Madaline and I moved aboard many years ago, we built a box to accept the newly installed refrigeration system. It was basically a good job, thickly insulated with several layers of polyurethane board. I lined the cavity with fiberglass and resin and then painted this surface with gloss white enamel. It looked wonderful. But as bad luck would have it, the resin out-gassed for almost a year. The odor permeated our food, making my wife most unhappy.

When *Caper* began cruising warm subtropic waters, we found the insulation still inadequate. I added more layers of polyurethane board to the inside of the reefer box—the heat transfer was greatly reduced, thus decreasing our compressor on-time. Madaline was not, however, about to endure another year of food tasting like the product of a plastic molding shop.

We found some white floor tile with an adhesive backing—for us, the perfect liner material. We simply set the tiles in place and trimmed the cuts to fit with scissors. We sealed the inside corners with silicone rubber and the outside corners of the lid with white vinyl tape. In two hours, the job was done. There was no odor, and the tile makes a great vapor barrier.

Formica countertop material can also be used for this purpose. Secure it with contact cement. But when you live aboard at anchor, work space is very limited, and we decided the large sheets would be hard to handle. We found the tile approach more economical as well as easier.

The Spice Locker

Long ago, I built a spice locker for *Caper*'s galley. It's a square mahogany box with a hinged cover. The shelves are deep enough to accommodate spice jars and are equipped with fiddles. The locker is screwed to the bulkhead in the galley, and Madaline's spices are easily within her reach.

The door to the locker is built like a picture frame. Before we moved aboard, it held a pretty sailing scene. Now, it is our family photo album. Each year we receive updated wallet-sized school photographs of our grandchildren. We also assemble current snapshots of our children, and

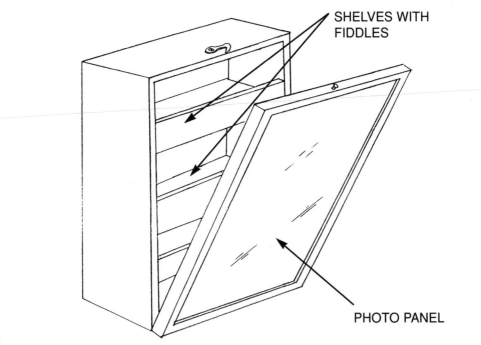

SHELVES WITH
FIDDLES

PHOTO PANEL

Fig. 2.3: The door of the spice locker is framed to hold a collage of family photographs.

Madaline creates a collage of them inside the door of her spice locker.

Dockside Pressurized Water

One of the problems of living aboard is keeping the water tank full. It invariably runs dry at dinnertime or in the morning when you are getting ready for work.

The solution to this dilemma, of course, is to tie into the dockside water, using a pressure regulator to reduce the line pressure at the hose bib. A tee and a check valve in the supply line from the boat's water tank to the distribution system allow you to pipe into a surface-mounted hose connector on the cabin side. A hose suitable for potable water can then be run from the dockside hose bib to the connector. The check valve prevents the water from the dockside source from flowing into the vessel's tanks, resulting in a flood. The Boat/US catalog generally carries a good diagram for such an installation. But the catalog doesn't tell you about the risk involved.

Even with a pressure regulator valve installed and set, a hose or hose clamp can fail in the distribution system to the galley or the head . An unrestricted flow at 15 psi can eventually sink your boat. For this reason, the dockside supply should be turned off every time you leave your boat. Problem was, Madaline and I could never remember to simply shut off the dockside faucet.

Our problem was solved in an unlikely manner. A number of companies that manufacture lawn sprinkler equipment now market metering valves that shut off after a preset number of gallons have passed through or a specified run time has elapsed. We feel that *Caper*'s bilge and pumps can safely handle 100 gallons of water and have set the control valve in one of those metering devices to pass that volume before shutting down.

Because the controller does not reset itself each time the dock faucet is turned off, it will eventually shut down the supply—probably in the middle of dinner or when you are getting ready for work. But that inconvenience sure beats a flooded or sunken boat.

4 THE HEAD

Acid Cleanout

If you sail in salt water, you will find that the discharge hose from the head eventually becomes plugged with use. The offending scale is a result of urine reacting with minerals in the seawater. It matters not if you flush the head directly out a through-hull or into a holding tank. Seawater is drawn into the head for flushing, and the end result is the same.

The situation can be controlled to some degree by a monthly treatment of acid. We use muriatic acid (a dilute form of hydrochloric acid), and others use vinegar. First, purge the lines of salt water by flushing a few gallons of fresh water through the head. With some fresh water still in the bottom of the bowl, pour in a pint of acid. *Caution: Do not add water to the acid!* Pump the acidic solution through the valving and into the discharge lines. Allow it to stand for 1 hour. At the end of this time, pump salt water through the head. The seawater will flush the neutralized acid and loosened scale out of the hose.

Incidentally, the minerals in seawater will combine

with the acid, rendering it ineffective, which is why fresh water must be used in the cleaning process.

This treatment is only a stopgap measure. Eventually, the hose must be removed and cleaned. I find the most effective means of clearing the hose is to flail it against the ground, which causes the brittle scale to break loose.

Odor Control

The marine head and the space in which it is located serve a natural human need—the elimination of waste. Unfortunately, and embarrassingly, this bodily function is often accompanied by odor. In the close confines of a boat, this can be an adverse situation. We have found that simply striking a match in the head works wonders. The unpleasant smell is quickly eliminated without the use of flowery scented aerosols.

5 THE FORWARD CABIN

Removable Bookshelf

Like most sailors, we are addicted to reading. Since storage space is at a premium, most of our books come from the local library if we're dockside. But there are a few books that we keep and go back to time after time. We needed space to accommodate the adventures of Travis McGee, *The Out Island Doctor,* and the poetry of Service.

Pearson Yachts saw fit to build wide shelves along the

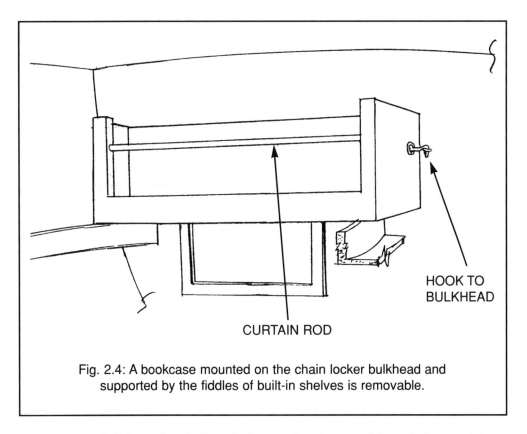

HOOK TO
BULKHEAD

CURTAIN ROD

Fig. 2.4: A bookcase mounted on the chain locker bulkhead and supported by the fiddles of built-in shelves is removable.

full length of *Caper's* forward cabin and faced them with high fiddles. Although they may have been designed for books, these shelves are where we keep most of our clothing (in the Keys, shorts and T-shirts are the traditional mode of dress). To accommodate our library, I built a removable bookshelf that rests on the fiddles of the built-in shelves and secures to the chainlocker bulkhead with chrome-plated hooks and eyes. The ends of the shelf are capped, and a 2-inch-high fiddle runs across the front. A spring-loaded brass curtain rod fits into holes counterbored in the end caps of the shelf to prevent the books from flying out in heavy seas. I used solid mahogany to match the interior of our home, but any wood will suffice. Resting easily on the two built-in fiddles, the removable bookshelf is high enough above the berth to clear even my size-twelve feet. When we need access to the chain locker, we simply release the two hooks and shift the bookshelf out of the way.

Chain Locker Doors

Speaking of the chain locker, it is wise to fasten screening inside the chain locker door to cover the ventilation holes. It's amazing how many insects otherwise find their way down the deck pipe, into the locker, and finally into the forward berth.

The doors of hanging lockers are usually vented at the top, solving only half of the problem of providing adequate air flow. Vents should also be installed at the bottom of the locker, as close as possible to the cabin sole. Having two sets of vents allows a convective air flow to circulate through the locker. Most marine suppliers sell teak louvers that are excellent for this purpose.

6 THE COMPANIONWAY

Security Doors

We have always admired boats that have been fitted with companionway doors. When we purchased our yawl, she came outfitted with a pair of louvered doors set into a U-shaped frame. The frame slid down into the dropboard track. This arrangement suited us nicely for a few years, but when we began to talk of living aboard, security became a factor.

Caper's new doors were built up from a pair of core sheets of 18-gauge stainless steel. Rectangular holes were cut in each metal panel to allow a window in the bottom and a screen in the top. Boards were planed down to 3/8-

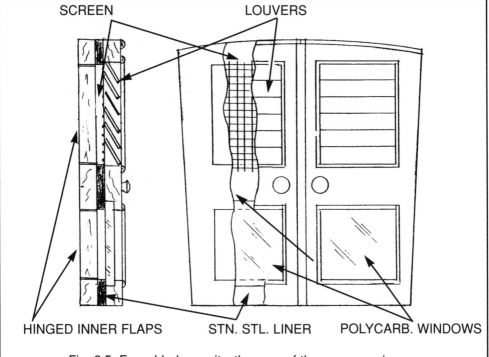

SCREEN   LOUVERS

HINGED INNER FLAPS   STN. STL. LINER   POLYCARB. WINDOWS

Fig. 2.5: For added security, the core of these companionway
doors is 18-gauge stainless steel.

inch thickness to face both sides of the metal and secured
with stainless steel self-tapping screws that were plugged.
The windows were fabricated from 1/4-inch polycarbonate,
and stainless steel mesh was used for screening, which was
spot-welded in place. Wooden louvers were fitted over the
screens, and hinged flaps were flush mounted inside both
screens and windows.

 With the doors complete, I removed the original stiles
from the companionway and replaced them with heavy
teak stiles, through-bolted in place over full-sized stainless
steel backing plates. Slip-joint motorbox hinges were used
to hang the doors on the new stiles so that the doors can be
removed whenever we desire. The companionway slide
closes over the doors and hooks to them to prevent its
being opened. A padlock hasp and staple is bolted to the
outside of the doors, and a slide bolt is installed inside.

 While someone with determination could still gain access to the cabin, the doors cannot be casually kicked in or forced. They would probably also suffice in storm conditions, but we still have the dropboards and their slot as a backup.

Screens

Here's an idea that we stole—with a few alterations—from Joe and Dean, the co-captains of *Drifter* out of Ashtabula, Ohio. We needed companionway screens, and theirs were very close to what we wanted.

We cut and carefully shaped wooden cross-sections to fit exactly the top and bottom of *Caper's* dropboard configuration. Each is about 2 inches high. The upper section is built with ears that engage the cabin top, thus keeping it in place. The companionway slide fits snugly over this part.

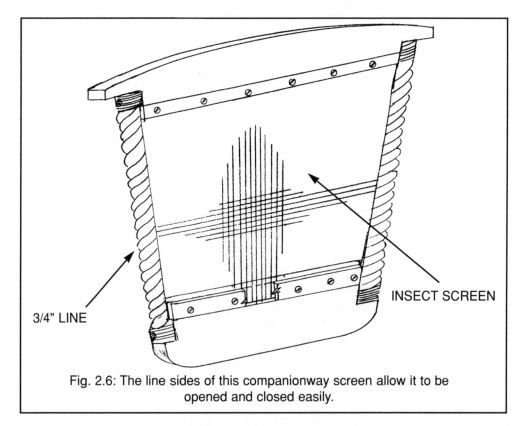

3/4" LINE

INSECT SCREEN

Fig. 2.6: The line sides of this companionway screen allow it to be opened and closed easily.

We carefully measured and cut two pieces of 3/4-inch line, seized their ends, and screwed them into notches in the ends of the upper and lower frame pieces. These lines form the sides of the screen frame and fit into the dropboard slides. We then screwed a piece of plastic insect screen into grooves in the upper and lower frame pieces and covered the raw edges with screwed-down battens. The job was completed by stitching the screen to the lines on the sides.

The finished assembly is set into the dropboard track. To open the screen we lift the lower wooden stringer up; the lines disengage from the grooves, but the upper section is held in place by the slide. To close the screen, we set the bottom back in place and run our hands down the lines—they reseat themselves easily.

The plastic inserts for the companionway mentioned in "Cold Days, Bright Cabins" (Chapter II) are the cool-weather counterparts to these screens.

The Emergency Knife

One blustery night, *Caper* and I nearly came to grief in Longboat Pass merely because I had neglected to carry a knife in my pocket and could not find one when I needed it.

The next morning, I remedied the situation. Years before, my father had fashioned a sheath knife from high-quality tool steel. It holds a fine edge. I mounted Dad's old blade just inside the companionway. It's like a nuclear submarine,—I hope that I never need it, but it's always there.

7 IN THE BILGE

Cleaning

Laura Berg aboard *L'Avinier* must be a magnificent
boatwife. When she is frustrated, she cleans the boat. As a
result, she gave us a good tip. The absorbency of diapers
make them excellent for soaking up grungy bilgewater.

For scrubbing a bilge after an oil or diesel spill, liquid
garage floor cleaner works very well. It emulsifies the oil
without needing to be heated the way many engine de-
greasers do.

A tablespoon of trisodium phosphate (TSP) in the bilgewater keeps it smelling fresh.

Of course, any bilge-cleaning operation must comply
with all applicable environmental regulations.

Down Cellar

During our sailing years on the Great Lakes, we found that
the chilly temperatures of those sweetwater seas of the
north made the bilge a fine cold storage locker to augment
our icebox. We fit a stainless steel mesh basket with U-tabs
that kept it hanging securely to the top of the centerboard
trunk. It held our supply of potatoes, onions, and the like.

We also crafted an energy-free wine cooler from a
short length of large-diameter plastic pipe capped at one
end. We fitted it with a hook to hang vertically into the
bilge.

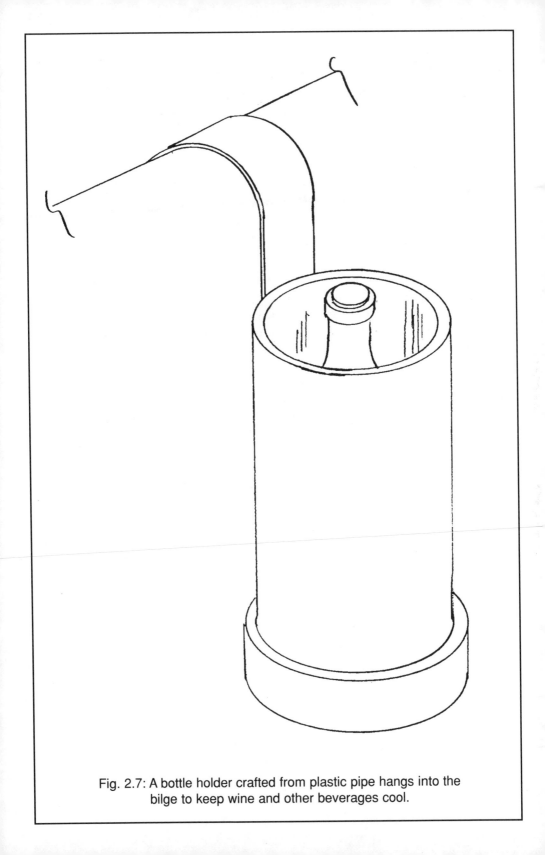

Fig. 2.7: A bottle holder crafted from plastic pipe hangs into the bilge to keep wine and other beverages cool.

8 WINTERIZING WATER TANKS

One of the hateful chores of sailing up north is laying up for the winter. We had problems draining the water tank and bought a nontoxic antifreeze from a marine supply. The following spring, the water always tasted awful, and we had to flush the tank and lines several times.

Ed Winkler of *Windhover* gave us an obvious solution. "Drain the tank," he said with a grin. "Then go buy a quart of cheap vodka and pour it into the tank. It will go into solution with the little remaining water and prevent it from freezing. And you can drink it without gagging next spring."

Naturally, it works! And a quart of booze doesn't make a very strong drink when it's diluted with 40 gallons of water.

The Auxiliary

1 DIESEL ENGINES

Safe Starts

Never use ether to help start a reluctant diesel. This highly volatile fuel in combination with the diesel's high compression can cause severe damage to the engine.

Jerry Miller of Glades Boat Storage suggests using WD-40 as an alternative. It has far less potential for causing an explosion within the cylinders.

Engine Shutdown

After a diesel has been run, it should be allowed to idle— and cool down—for just a few minutes before it is shut off. A hot engine causes the cooling water to boil in the area near the valves, resulting in burned valve seats.

Jury-rigged Fuel

In an emergency, an acceptable fuel for a diesel engine can be blended by mixing one part of motor oil with four parts of kerosene.

Troubleshooting Hints

These hints for spotting signs of trouble came to me from Jim Kline, a diesel mechanic and sailing liveaboard down in the Florida Keys.

If the crankcase oil smells like diesel, it's likely that there's a leak in the fuel pump diaphragm.

White smoke from the exhaust upon start-up is a sign of unburned fuel, indicating low compression.

Raw fuel floating on the water after start-up is a sign of "dribbling" injectors. The fuel leaks down the cylinder walls, stripping away lubricating oil, which results in scored cylinder walls.

Engine Waterpumps

If your engine overheats, there are the obvious items to check: thermostat, waterpump impeller, hoses and gaskets for leaks, engine and heat exchanger for blockages. Here's another possibility: The seals on the raw-water pump may be leaking. This malfunction is minimal at lower engine speeds, but as the rpm's increase, so does the leakage across the seals.

To check for this problem, disconnect the hose from the discharge side of the pump. Start the engine, and slowly advance the throttle. The flow rate from the pump should steadily increase. If the seals are faulty, the flow suddenly begins to decline as the engine runs progressively faster. Obviously, the engine should be run for only a very short time in this manner.

Changing the Oil

Changing the oil on any auxiliary, gas or diesel, is about as much fun as undergoing a root canal. Using one of those little hand pumps, I've managed to sling dirty oil all over the cabin, annoy my wife, and invent a whole new vocabulary in profanity.

Aboard *Lady Galadriel,* Irwin Schmitt, my sailing buddy from the Chesapeake Bay, has developed a scheme that takes all the agony out of this maintenance ordeal.

With the proper equipment—a means of drawing even a partial vacuum—this is the way to go. The equipment can be a high-vacuum pump or even a good ejector. Irwin uses an empty refrigerant bottle, but a small LPG tank does just as well. Pump a vacuum onto the container and close off its valve. To the valve attach a small-diameter hose that fits down into the engine's dip-stick tube. Insert the hose and open the valve. The vacuum bottle sucks the crankcase dry in moments.

My method is a little more traditional. After years of delaying this job until some day when Madaline was away from the boat and I hated myself, I installed a valve on the crankcase drain and attached a long hose to the valve. I insert the hose into the mouth of an old antifreeze jug that neatly fits into *Caper*'s bilge, open the valve—and then sit back and sip a cup of coffee. When my coffee break is over, I close the valve, wipe the hose clean and secure it, and then retrieve the jug full of old oil.

Crankcase Condensate

Prior to living aboard, we lived in a house and sailed only during the summer. Each autumn, we laid *Caper* up in Chet Kuhn's boatyard on Sodus Bay, along Lake Ontario's south shore. One winter was warm and wet. In the spring, when I checked the engine, the crankcase was full of oil and water! Fearing the worst, I explained the problem to Chet.

"Not to worry," he said. "I see a lot of that. The warm wet air flows into the engine; the moisture condenses on the cold blocks and settles into the crankcases. If this goes on day after day, pretty soon you've got nearly as much water as oil. Drain the engine, and pour in some fresh oil. She'll be okay." Sure enough, the old Atomic 4 then ran for several years.

2 BATTERIES

For a Long Life

We are typical of most cruising sailors—we spend much of our time at anchor. Some of my time on the hook is devoted to watching the condition of the batteries. This is simply because we feel, like many others, that cruising without refrigeration is uncivilized. And refrigeration is the major drain on the battery bank.

Over the past several years, I have developed a schedule for our battery bank that works for us. Our number 1 and number 2 batteries are both deep cycle, the type that can be drawn far down repeatedly without damage to the plates. They are connected to the boat's electrical system through the battery selector switch.

Each morning, I switch from one battery to the other, commencing with number 1 on the first of the month. The designated battery starts the engine, drives the refrigeration, and powers the lights and VHF for the next twenty-four hours. Meanwhile, the other battery lies dormant. *Caper*'s diesel cranks easily, so I don't fear harming the deep-cycle batteries.

People who know batteries maintain that when cells are allowed to rest they regain a portion of their charge, and the life span is also extended. Giving ours regular breaks has worked well for us.

But we still carry a number 3 battery as an ace in the hole.

Chargers and Timers

Naturally, the batteries aboard your boat must be kept charged to be useful. In the slip, with shore power plugged in, the typical charger provides a constant flow of current to the battery bank. But this ongoing trickle charge actually shortens the life span of the battery that it is trying to maintain.

We installed a switch on the circuit feeding 110-volt AC power to the charger. We turn the switch off every morning when we are aboard and reactivate it in the evening. Recently, I installed a 24-hour timer that does the job for us.

When we are away from the boat for an extended period, all the 12-volt DC systems are shut down except for the bilgepumps; they must remain operational. The timer is reset to provide a minimal charge time of up to an hour once or twice a day to meet this small but crucial load.

Charging Batteries at Anchor

Dennis Scully of *Pioneer Spirit* suggested that whenever we run the auxiliary at anchor to charge the batteries, we put the engine in gear—in reverse. Diesels build up carbon deposits when they are run with no load.

Just be certain that your anchor is well set, especially in a crowded harbor. Since most boats crab to port or starboard in reverse, it's better to risk a bit of carbon in close quarters.

IV

Boatwright Skills

1
CANVAS WORK

2
JOINERY

1 CANVAS WORK

Maintenance

Acrilan awnings, bimini tops, and the like eventually lose their waterproofing. Applying a silicone spray to the fabric works for a while, but an application of Thompson's Waterseal lasts at least one season.

Andy McCloud of *Mercedes II* told me that when snap fasteners on awnings and dodgers become hard to work, he smears a dab of petroleum jelly on the inside of the snap. The jelly lubricates the tiny spring, providing it freedom of motion once again.

The following tip was gleaned from a canvas repair shop in St. Petersburg, Florida. Many sail covers use quarter-turn fasteners to secure the closure around the boom. After a few years, the tang of the fasteners pulls through the material. New fasteners can be installed, but they should be the surface-mounted type set on a flange with two holes for mounting screws. Rivet the new fittings in place using studs from snap fasteners. The tubular shank can be easily spread using a small Phillips-head screwdriver.

When passing a line through a grommet, do as the fishermen do: Put a loop in it. A bight will pass through a hole more readily than a standing end.

If the straps on your bimini hum in the wind, unhook them, twist each strap one turn, and then resnap them. This simple act changes the frequency of vibration and the straps fall silent.

Dodgers

The clear plastic material used for dodger windows has a rather short life span when constantly exposed to the rays of the sun. It becomes cloudy and brittle. Our first set of windows lasted only two years in the Florida sun. Then we learned how to preserve the replacement units.

We made covers—Bob Trudell of *Waymar* calls his diapers—of blue Acrilan for each of the dodger windows. They overlap onto the matching fabric of the dodger about 1 inch all around, creating a light seal and providing fastening space. Each is secured with snaps and Velcro tape. We remove them only when we leave the dock or during times of extremely high winds. We even use them when we're at anchor in one place for a number of days.

The current set of windows is now nine years old and has yet to show signs of deterioration.

2 JOINERY

A Custom-blended Filler

Caper was remodeled quite extensively when we moved aboard. We were very fortunate; my good friend Eric Tinney is a master carpenter, and he devoted an entire winter to helping me when he could have been tinkering with his *Shared Pleasure*.

We built a set of lockers where the pilot berth used to be. Since the yawl's cabin is mahogany, we used the same wood for the locker front and door frames. Eric is meticulous and insisted that even the nail holes be filled with a matching color. Here's how he did it.

Using a piece of fine sandpaper, he sanded the butt end of a piece of wood cut from the board on which we were working. He collected the sanding dust onto a sheet of white paper. When a sufficient pile had accumulated, he mixed it thoroughly with carpenter's glue into a thick slurry and then sealed the nail holes with the compound. When it was dry, he sanded the board smooth. The nail holes are barely visible.

Seating Wooden Plugs

When the locker door front was completed, we set it in place and fastened it with brass screws. Plug and mallet in hand, I reached for the squeeze bottle of glue to begin plugging the holes.

"No, you don't," said Eric. "A plug is set in varnish. Then it can be removed if you ever need to remove or tighten the screw beneath it. Varnish will let the plug break out clean—glue will not—and the varnish is always waterproof."

Ventilated Locker Doors

Two of the locker doors that Eric built are quite large, about 2 feet square. I wanted them to be an attractive part of the cabin, and Madaline insisted that they be ventilated since she would be storing clothes and bedding behind them and was concerned about mildew.

Eric made the doors to resemble a pair of wooden picture frames. They are rabbeted around the outer perimeter to set into the doorfront and around the inside to receive a panel of caning.

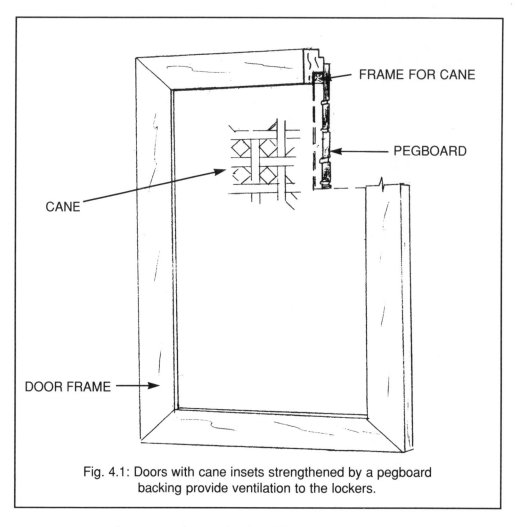

FRAME FOR CANE

PEGBOARD

CANE

DOOR FRAME

Fig. 4.1: Doors with cane insets strengthened by a pegboard backing provide ventilation to the lockers.

These panels are built of lightweight wooden frames that fit loosely into the door cavities. We soaked the caning in water overnight before tacking it onto the frames. As the cane dried, it shrank tightly across the front of the doors. Bamboo cane, incidentally, is immune to mildew.

Although handsome and well ventilated, initially the doors were not strong enough to withstand continued use aboard a cruising sailboat. The problem was solved by screwing pegboard to the back of the doors. The pegboard made them rigid but still allowed plenty of air to flow into the lockers. We painted the surface of the pegboard behind the caning a flat black. It is virtually invisible.

Quick and Easy Patterns

An old gent named Nick was building a boat, and I spent a few days helping him.

Whenever he needed a pattern made, he went to his wood supply and dug out a handful of long narrow strips of 1/4-inch plywood. He cut these into lengths that would fit the outline of the part he wanted and fastened them together with a screw gun. When he was finished, he would dismantle the parts and save them for the next pattern.

3 MARLINESPIKE

One winter in a dead-end job, I bought a book on knots to help pass the time. Generally, I'm pretty good at marlinespike. But now and then I still have trouble remembering the bowline when the wind is cranking, it's the middle of the night, and I'm shivering on deck trying to add a spring-line.

The Prusik Knot

One of the handiest knots that I've seen in a long while came to me from Jim Bradley of *Sawadi'i*. A climber's knot called the prusik, it can be used to secure a flag halyard to a shroud, to make an adjustable tension line, or in pairs to create "steps" for your feet for emergency mast climbing.

To tie the prusik, take two loops around the object you are tying, bring the free end back, and tuck it through

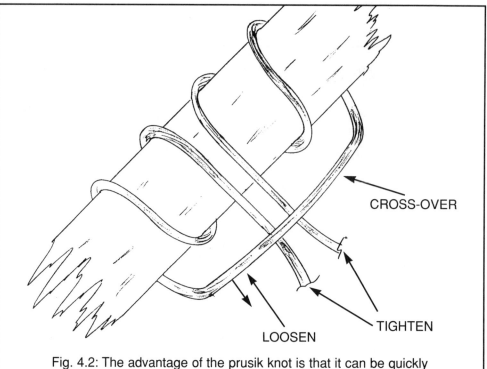

CROSS-OVER

LOOSEN

TIGHTEN

Fig. 4.2: The advantage of the prusik knot is that it can be quickly released and reset.

twice. When the knot is pulled tight, the turns should rest evenly against the object. No doubt you're confused by now, so look at my sketch—it may help.

This knot is a constrictor. Its advantage is that it can be released quickly and reset by rotating the cross-over portion of the knot.

The Turk's Head

Here's another constrictor knot, but it serves a totally different purpose—once set, it's on for keeps. The Turk's head is usually considered a strictly decorative knot, but we have used it for many purposes. Its attractive appearance just enhances its usefulness.

Caper's navigation lights are mounted where the bow pulpit is joined by a bracing stanchion on each side of the bow. The jibs chafed and wore on the fixtures until Turk's heads around the pulpit tubing provided a neat form of chafing gear. Four of these knots are used on each of the rigging rollers to hold the halves tightly together. I've even used two of them as stoppers for the mizzen traveler that runs across the stern pulpit.

There are many books of knots that describe how to tie the Turk's head far better than I can. But I urge you to try some aboard your boat; the Turk's head is a handy knot.

The Fisherman's Knot

I've had trouble tying two dissimilar lines together, especially if one is polypropylene. Lines made of this material tend to slip out of sheet bends at embarrassing moments. As a reliable alternative, I've settled on the fisherman's knot.

Tie an overhand knot in the end of one of the lines that you want to join together. Pass the standing end of the second line through the bight formed by this overhand knot. Now tie an overhand knot in the second line, enclosing the first line in its bight. Pull the individual knots tight, and then draw them together.

If the knot stays in place for a long period of time and gets wet, it may become a hatchet knot: You need a hatchet to get the two lines apart.

4 ELECTRICAL ISSUES

A Waterproof Splice

Everyone knows that electricity and water are not good companions. But they must coexist on a boat. Nels Gustafson of *Leagasea* taught me this trick.

A waterproof wire splice can be accomplished in a neat inexpensive manner. Prepare your splice using a regular crimp-style butt fitting. Before inserting the wires into the fitting, squirt it full of silicone rubber. Then insert the wires and make the crimps as normal. Wipe off the bit of silicone that oozes out. As soon as the silicone is set, you have a waterproof joint.

This is a good technique to use when installing bilge-pumps.

Low-Amperage Anchor Light

Many are the boats that have bled a battery dead overnight burning an anchor light from the masthead, because anchor lights are notorious energy hogs. There are several alternatives on the market, including the old faithful kerosene lantern. We used one for years and still carry it as a standby. But Pete Berg of *L'Avenier* showed me his homemade anchor light, and I happily copied it. The total cost can amount to less than five dollars.

Radio Shack sells a 12-volt bulb that consumes just 0.075 amps! The part number is 272-1143, and the bulbs come in a packet of two. Radio Shack also sells a socket to match the bulb. Solder a pair of wires to the socket, and connect a 12-volt DC plug to the other end. Screw in the bulb, plug the cord into a cockpit 12-volt socket, and you have a usable light.

Now comes the difficult part—you need a lens to direct the light rays. Search around until you locate a small cut-glass saltshaker or bottle. This is your Fresnel lens (Mr. Fresnel didn't pronounce the S in his name, by the way). The more facets on the saltshaker, the more efficient the light is. We purchased a set of miniature shakers about 1 1/2 inches high with a diagonal pattern all the way around. Unscrew the cap and fit the lamp socket into the neck of the shaker, positioning the lamp's filament about halfway into the container. Then seal the assembly with silicone rubber. Someday the lamp will burn out, and you must be able to replace it. Make a bale out of a length of light-gauge wire so that you can hoist the light on a flag halyard. Plug the light in, and your battery won't even know that it is lit!

We have been able to see *Caper*'s anchor light from well over a mile off with no difficulty. I believe that this unit is fully capable of being spotted within a 2-mile range in a fair test. It is much brighter than our old lantern.

5 THE FINISHING TOUCH: THE SISTERHOOD OF BRIGHTWORK

Madaline and I have an agreement—she doesn't touch the wrenches, and I don't touch the paintbrushes. The following story tells how this came to be. The main character in this yarn, Jan, is actually a composite of Memmit Crane of *Seawind*, Carol Walker of *Grand Turk*, and Nancy Greiner—the lady varnisher of Big Boat Row.

In spite of layers of dirt and obvious signs of misuse, *Windward*'s beauty was still obvious. "A lovely lady fallen upon hard times," I thought. A ketch rig, she was built in a Far East yard and sailed to the States on her own bottom by a wealthy owner. But that was long ago. Since then, she had seen seven kinds of hell in the charter trade. Now a new owner was giving her a second lease on life.

I was spending two weeks overhauling her rigging and electrical system. My technical skills were not in high demand, so like many of our liveaboard neighbors, I was in the yacht repair business. (Madaline wore nurses' whites and had quickly signed on at a local hospital.)

As I came up *Windward*'s companionway one fine clear morning, I saw Jan's long legs swing over the rail. "I'm here to refinish the brightwork," she announced.

In her shoreside incarnation, Jan had been an executive secretary. Now she dresses for work in cut-off jeans and an old shirt. She says she's much happier—and earns more money. The demand for her varnishing skills among the captains of the gold-platers out along Big Boat Row is great. Jan is among the first to admit that she is very good at her craft. "I'm not your typical slop-on-the-varnish type," she says proudly. "Anybody can lay on varnish. It's all those little extra touches that make the overall result something special."

Windward's teak was darkened, and the finish was dull—where it wasn't worn completely away. "I'll have to strip it all off," Jan commented.

"That should take almost a gallon of paint remover," I volunteered.

"One never uses chemical stripper on teak," was the haughty reply. "It will attack the softer fibers of the wood, leaving only the harder grain intact. The end result is a wavy, uneven surface. Why, just look at Jack's trawler across the dock."

Sure enough, the trawler's brightwork resembled a highly finished washboard.

"I always use an electric hot-air gun," Jan said. "It softens the old finish without charring the wood. Then I can easily scrape the varnish off."

In a few days, all of *Windward*'s teak was stripped bare. Jan proceeded to bleach the wood to its natural golden color with oxalic acid, one of the prime constituents of most teak cleaners. After briskly but carefully scrubbing the teak with bronze wool, she neutralized the acid with an application of borax and water. This step was followed by several rinses with fresh water from the dockside hose.

While rigging my bosun's chair, I couldn't resist making conversation. "You've really got a lot of sanding to do now."

"There'll be no sanding done yet," she chided me. "That wood grain is standing up and open just as it is—absolutely perfect for receiving a fifty-fifty coat of varnish and thinner for a sealant. It will wick down through the pores of the teak much more thoroughly than after a sanding. Sanding lays the fibers down, just like brushing a dog's fur smooth and flat. Also, the heat generated by the abrasion would bring the teak's natural oils to the surface, preventing a good bond between the wood and the varnish."

"Before I start, I'll mask the surrounding surfaces. I usually use the new easy-off masking tape because its adhesive won't migrate into the base material, and I don't have to use acetone and a putty knife to scrape off the tape when I'm finished. It lifts off as nice as can be. But the tape salesman at the boat show told me to leave it on for only a few days out in the full sun. Just recently, I've discovered that regular black vinyl electrical tape is great for some masking jobs. It doesn't stick very well, but it stretches and follows curved lines really smoothly."

Jan had barely finished masking when Mike, her husband, strolled down the dock. He's a teacher turned diver.

"Watch me get her goin'," he said, with a twinkle in his Irish eyes. "Hey, me darlin'," he roared. "Do ye want me to fetch that old varnish that I bought at the chandlery sale last year?"

"You know darned well that I wouldn't use that gloppy mess on this lovely teak," she shot back. "So you can just march yourself up to the van and carry down those two new quarts of varnish for me."

This time, I sat quietly on the dock to watch the artisan at work. She popped the lid on one of the cans and poured a small amount through a paint strainer into a plastic container. "You never work straight from the can; it contaminates the varnish. Take only what you need, straining it, and use a clean container every time. I like these little margarine tubs, but the cardboard cups the paint store sells also work. The first two coats should be thinned fifty-fifty and seventy-five–twenty-five. Later applications can be made full strength."

Picking up the varnish can, Jan tilted the lid against the rim of the container at the point farthest from her. Taking a deep breath, she exhaled into the can, dropped the lid into place, and quickly tapped it home.

"Aha," I crowed, "I know what you did just then. You replaced the oxygen-rich air with carbon dioxide, which is relatively inert."

"If you say so, Mister Mechanic," she replied with a grin. "I only know that a film won't form over the surface of the varnish now."

When she brought out her brush, I was appalled. "You're using one of those cheap things?" I jeered. It was a plastic foam brush on a wood handle.

"This is the best there is," she answered. "These brushes don't lose bristles, leave no brush marks, and can be tossed when I'm finished. Besides, I save on my labor—and money—by not cleaning brushes. You would be surprised how much a project proper brush cleaning is."

Jan was aboard the ketch before I arrived the next morning. She was cutting away at the first coat with a palm sander—a husky model built for the trades. I picked up a pad of the spent sandpaper. It was 220 grit. She was doing a lightning fast job on the flat and convex surfaces. Later, from my perch in the mizzen spreaders, I watched as she wrapped a similar piece of new abrasive paper around a wooden block. She used it to sand concave curves and hard-to-reach places.

"Your hands are too flexible," she explained later over break-time coffee. "Without the block, they would wear the softer wood away, just like stripper. The block spans across the heavy grains, leaving the sanded surface smooth and flat."

A rainsquall hit that night, and the next morning was hot and humid. Jan stopped by to tell me that she wouldn't be working that day. "The varnish wouldn't dry properly, and it might orange peel. I'll do my laundry instead."

The following day, Jan commenced with coat number three, laying the varnish down uncut. She sanded between applications using the palm sander and the wooden block, again with 220-grit paper. On subsequent coats, she water-sanded lightly with 400-grit wet-or-dry paper. The fourth coat looked good to me, but she kept going for a total of six. *Windward*'s brightwork had the sheen of fine furniture when Jan peeled away the masking tape.

Later, I noticed that Madaline was spending a while each evening chatting with Jan. "Woman talk," I said to myself. I had found a full-time job and had somewhat re-gretfully given up my yacht service venture. My taking the new job, however, allowed Madaline to cut back on her hours.

Eventually, varnishing time rolled around aboard *Caper*. "I'm doing the brightwork this year," my spouse an-nounced. "Jan has been telling me how to do it. She's cer-tain that women are better varnishers than men. You are not really very careful, you know. And besides, I have more time now."

She also informed me what she wanted for her birthday—a palm sander. "And not one of those rinky-dinks from the outlet store." She even knew the manufacturer and model number.

And so the process that I saw used on *Windward*'s brightwork was now repeated on *Caper*'s, with identical results.

These events took place some years ago. Since then, Madaline's refinishing of the brightwork has become an annual onboard ritual. Here in Florida under the blazing subtropic sun, two coats preceded by a heavy sanding are all that the woodwork needs to restore the radiance. The first coat is thinned, but the next is laid down full strength after a thorough wet sanding. Madaline has developed a technique all her own. After every sanding, she wipes the wood clean using a cloth soaked in alcohol. "A tack rag sometimes leaves a residue," she says. "The alcohol evaporates quickly so that you can varnish the cleaned area immediately."

Last week, I was on deck doing a minor chore when Ted came by for a visit. He's a new liveaboard but spent thirty years operating his own boatyard. Obviously, the man knows a bit about boats. In the course of the conversation, I mentioned that *Caper* was more than a quarter century old. "She can't be," he insisted. "She looks too good to be that age, especially her teak." I took that to be the ultimate compliment to my wife's hard work and skill.

So this is one professional's way to varnish the brightwork and keep it Bristol fashion. By now, I too am convinced that women are the better varnishers. They are generally much more meticulous than we menfolk. But now, my friend, it's up to you to convince The Lady You Sail With of this fact.

This story first appeared in *Coastal Cruising*, April 1992.

6 RIGGING

Truing a Mast

One of the most intimidating steps to getting ready to sail is setting up the mast. But it really isn't all that difficult.

Start by making certain that the mast is perpendicular to the deck. Bring a halyard down to a starboard stanchion or chainplate, and cleat it off when it touches. Swing the halyard to the port side of the vessel, and try to touch the corresponding fitting. If the halyard is loose, the mast leans to port and the starboard upper shroud should be tightened. If the halyard is too short to touch the port-side fitting, loosen the starboard upper and tighten the port. Continue this process until the halyard is equally taut to the fitting on each side. You now have two identical triangles with the mast forming a common side.

Now sight up the mast track. If it bends to one side or the other, loosen the offending lower shrouds and snug up their opposites.

Mast rake is a matter of the vessel's design and the need for more or less weather helm. Rake is controlled by the fore- and back-stays.

While snug rigging is fine, do not draw the shrouds so tight that distortion of the cabin or hull occurs.

Jury-rigged Mast Stepping

An old gentleman once told me a hunting story. "It's so true I don't even have to lie about it," he said. So it is with this tale.

One spring weekend, most of the boats had been launched in Chet Kuhn's boatyard. But *Pendragon*'s mast

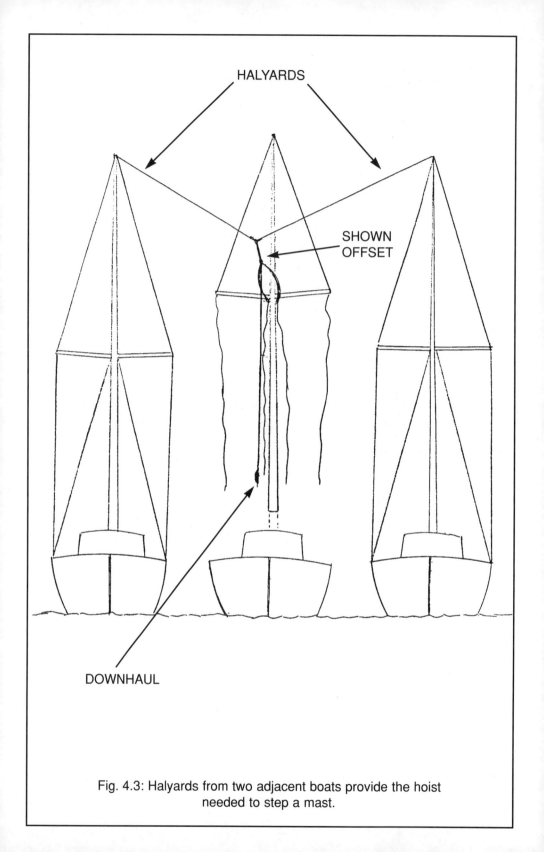

HALYARDS

SHOWN
OFFSET

DOWNHAUL

Fig. 4.3: Halyards from two adjacent boats provide the hoist
needed to step a mast.

hadn't been stepped yet, and Bill Marsh wanted to go sailing. Unfortunately, the crane was out of commission. The red sloop lay in her slip between *Caper* and Al Bernreuther's *Vintage*. Both these boats had their masts up and were rigged. *Pendragon*'s mast lay in X-frames atop the boat.

The three of us considered the situation for a while and determined that we could raise *Pendragon*'s mast. Al and I each ran a halyard over to Bill. He made them fast to the end of a line. Near the end of this line, he tied a bowline loosely around the mast just below the tangs of the lower shrouds. The remainder of the line was long enough to nearly reach the base of the mast.

Al and I began to winch in the halyards at an even pace. The mast came clear of the frames, and friends Alex Piccirilli and Tom Purdum stepped aboard to help Bill guide the spar. We shifted the boats slightly to align all the mast steps and continued to crank. When the mast was vertical, Al and I eased the halyards, with some other folk tailing. The mast slid easily into its step. The loose end of the line securing the halyards was our downhaul.

Pendragon went sailing the next day.

V

On the Hard

1
PAINTING

2
THE HULL

1 PAINTING

Spicy Bottom Paint

The big-time paint companies belittle this notion. But it has been recommended to me by Paul from New Bedford, Lew from the Outer Banks, and Steve from Tampa Bay. All these men are commercial fishermen. All of them add cayenne pepper to their bottom paint (about 2 oz. of pepper per gallon of paint). They maintain that it keeps their boats' bottoms free of barnacles.

We have used the pepper treatment in our bottom paint ever since our first haulout in Florida a long while back. Our sailing grounds are in warm subtropic waters, and we haul out every second year. *Caper* has yet to grow her first barnacle since we began this practice. Maybe that's just a coincidence, but we doubt it.

Visible Through-hull Fittings

The very first time we hauled *Caper* in Florida, the yard foreman suggested that we paint her through-hull fittings with a paint different from the kind we used on the fiberglass hull. At that time, tin-based paints were still legal, and he felt that the extra protection they afforded would be worthwhile. So we launched *Caper* with a red bottom and white through-hulls.

It did not take me long to discover a second advantage to this color scheme. The white of the tin-based paint contrasted with the red background of *Caper*'s bottom paint, and when I dove to clean the bottom and check the fittings, the through-hulls were readily visible.

Tin-based paints are gone now, and I can seldom find

a small quantity of white bottom paint around the yard where we haul. I usually substitute blue, and it stands out just as sharply in the gin-clear waters of the Keys and islands. The contrast makes life a whole lot easier when you are looking for an engine water intake plugged with marine growth or a knotmeter fouled with fish line.

2 THE HULL

Caulking the Toerail

One winter, a Canadian sailor named Werner lived aboard *Pamparo*, just down the dock from us in St. Pete. He was restoring the elderly Rhodes Swiftsure to Bristol fashion.

Pamparo and *Caper* shared a common malady: chronic leaks at the deck-to-hull joint beneath the wooden toerail. Werner made things right aboard the elderly sloop, and I copied this project as soon as I saw how he did it.

Using a church key bottle opener, Werner scraped out any loose caulking, dirt, and bits of gelcoat from beneath each side of the teak toerail. He then masked along the hull and the toerail, leaving only a 1/8-inch gap between the strips of tape, and repeated this preparation along the inboard edge of the teak and the deck. He then laid a thin bead of 3M 5200 compound as caulking into the wood and fiberglass interface. Placing a plastic bag over his hand for protection, Werner ran his forefinger along the bead, forcing the caulking into the crevices and smoothing the surface. He shifted the bag as he worked and changed when it became loaded with excess material. When the masking tape was stripped away, Werner had a neat concave strip of caulk all along the edges of each toerail.

Cleaning the Mustache

The southern waterways of the United States are frequently a rich brown color. While the tone adds to the romance of the Spanish-moss settings, the tannin-saturated water is a bane to boaters. It causes a distinctive brown mustachelike stain on the bow of any vessel running through it.

I worked in a boatyard one winter. A large power yacht was hauled for a bottom job, to replace the zincs and undergo the usual cosmetics. Since I was responsible for her, I asked the yard boss what cleaner to use to remove the twin smudges from the bow.

"Well, here's what we use," he said, picking up a bottle of specially formulated cleaner. "But if it were my boat, I'd use toilet bowl cleaner. It's virtually the same compound, but it is a whole lot cheaper."

Waxing Made Easy

It was one of those rare springtime days along the Great Lakes. It was hot! And there I was, waxing the hull before launching the boat—but the sun was baking the wax onto the gelcoat before I could get back to buff it out with a soft cloth. The more I struggled with the wax, the worse the job looked. Smears and streaks kept reappearing, and my cloth bogged down in the mess.

Alex Piccirilli of *Ruthie-O* came wandering by and took pity on me. "Rest a minute, Joe," he said. "I'll be right back."

He soon returned carrying a can of turpentine and a large square of cheesecloth. Wetting the cheesecloth with the turpentine, he wiped down the waxed hull. The cloth absorbed most of the heavy mass of polish, but an even film remained.

"Now buff that out," Alex instructed me.

I did, and it was amazingly easy. The gelcoat glistened with highlights in the afternoon sun.

We have used this trick ever after. Recently, though, we have substituted mineral spirits with equally pleasing results.

Applying Graphics

Walking down the dock one day, I came upon our neighbor, Dayton Lovelein, sitting on his finger pier. He was applying new state registry numbers on *High Roller*.

These were not the individual digits and letters sold in every hardware store, but graphics coordinated to match the vessel's color scheme. They included a pleasing shadowing in a contrasting shade, which gave them a three-dimensional effect. The numbers were all on a single sheet for easy application, but the shadows were on a separate sheet. Aligning the two didn't seem like an easy task.

"Looks like a helluva job," I remarked.

"Not too bad," Dayton replied. "The adhesive is waterproof, so I just wet the surface with a weak soap solution. I can slide the graphics around 'til everything is positioned just right. Then I simply squeegee out the water."

VI

Accessories

VI

Accessories

1
THE DINGHY

1 THE DINGHY

Most sailors have a love-hate relationship with their dinghy. A dinghy is indispensable—but what on earth do you do with it?

Towing

If you simply must trail your dinghy when under way, use two lines, preferably made fast to different stern cleats. We know of one expensive tender that was lost on a long Gulf of Mexico passage when the single towline parted, chafed through, or simply came loose.

String floats along the towlines. Doing so can save you the unpleasant task of diving to unwrap the line from your boat's propeller. An alternative is to use polypropylene water-ski rope, which floats, but polypropylene lacks the shock-absorbing elasticity of nylon.

Hauling the dink out of the water and lashing it to the foredeck is still the best procedure during an open-water crossing or a storm. Another boat that we know lost its dinghy to towing during the Storm of the Century even with two towlines rigged.

Oar and Oarlock Storage

When we purchased *Caper*, her tender was included as part of the deal—for which we are very thankful. But there was no stowage place aboard the dink for the oars or oarlocks. I kept the oars in *Caper*'s lazarette—usually beneath sails, lifejackets, and spare docklines. The oarlocks migrated

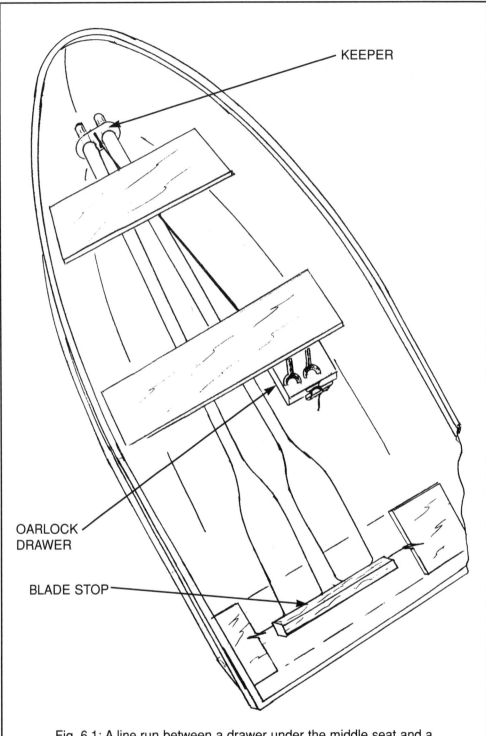

KEEPER

OARLOCK
DRAWER

BLADE STOP

Fig. 6.1: A line run between a drawer under the middle seat and a custom-fit keeper over the oar handles holds the oarlocks and oars securely in place.

from lockers to junk drawers and back. Finally, I resolved to find some other location.

Beneath the middle seat of the dink I built a small drawer with cavities cut to store the oarlocks. On the face of the drawer in place of a knob I screwed a small cleat, which serves a second purpose. The drawer opens aft.

I stowed the oars beneath the seats with the blade tips placed against the transom. A piece of wood trim mounted horizontally along the transom holds the blades down.

Next, I cut a rectangular piece of polycarbonate and bored two holes in it, on the long axis, each large enough to clear the oar handles but small enough to stop against the greater diameter of the looms. Two smaller holes accept a light nylon line, which I tie to this plastic keeper. After slipping the keeper over the oar handles, I run the line aft and make it fast to the cleat on the drawer. This line holds the drawer shut and secures the oars at the same time.

Over the past several years, *Caper* has cruised thousands of miles and been through her share of blows. And the oars are always in place, ready and waiting to use.

Afloat, but Barnacle Free

Ambrey was down Sailfish Dock from *Caper* for a couple of years. Fred Neal often kept his inflatable dinghy in the water for a period of time, but he never had to scrape barnacles off its bottom. How did he manage to keep the dink clean? He had a simple trick.

Whenever Fred came back in with the dink, he retrieved three old partially inflated inner tubes that he kept stashed under the dock. One he stuffed under the tender's bow and the other two went under its stern—one each port and starboard. The tubes kept the craft's bottom just free of the water's surface.

Bilge Keels for Sailing Dinghies

Our dinghy is an elderly but wonderfully sound 8-foot Dyer
Dhow. She rows like a dream, moves quickly with only a
2-horsepower outboard, and stows easily on stern davits. I
had always wanted to give her a sailing rig, and a few years
ago, I did.

It was basically a simple proposition. I purchased a do-
it-yourself kit for a spritsail. Building a rudder and tiller
out of available pine was no problem. But I did not want to
violate the hull's integrity by cutting in a daggerboard slot.

I remembered a conversation I once had with John
Fessenmeyer of the Old Wooden Boat Works of Bradenton,
Florida. John builds a beautiful sailing dink that uses nei-
ther daggerboard nor centerboard. He discovered that a
simple 6-inch-deep keel serves very adequately.

Never being one to copy blatantly if I can make a wee

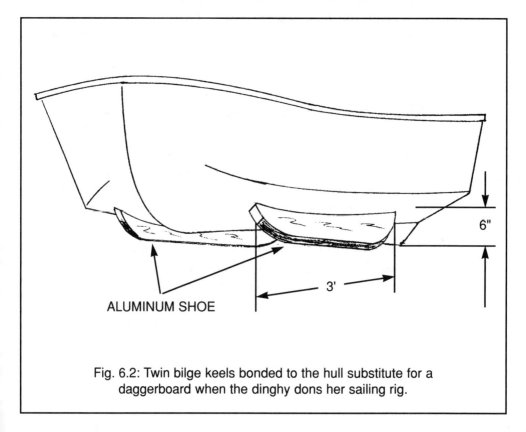

ALUMINUM SHOE

6"

3'

Fig. 6.2: Twin bilge keels bonded to the hull substitute for a
daggerboard when the dinghy dons her sailing rig.

modification, I added a pair of similar-sized bilge keels to our tender. They are bonded to the gelcoat with epoxy resin but are not fiberglassed in place. Cut from 3/4-inch pine, they are 3 feet long. At the fore and after ends, they are 6 inches deep, but because of the dinghy's bottom configuration are only about 4 inches amidships. I capped the keels with an aluminum strip for abrasion resistance.

I'm pleased to report that in a decent breeze our dink points as close to the wind as several others that I have sailed with. Between the two keels and her square chine, she makes little leeway. The bilge keels also protect the bottom from taking a beating on coral out in the Bahamas.

Incidentally, the loose-footed spritsail tacks nicely, sheets in and out, and even reefs quickly—by dropping the sprit. The mast and sprit stow along *Caper*'s mizzen shrouds but could be built in pieces and nest in the dink. And with 45 square feet of sail, the acceleration is awesome!

Umbrellas

Madaline finds carrying an old umbrella in the dinghy a good idea.

When the outboard is powering the tender, she rides in the bow seat. Thus, when chop builds in an anchorage, she receives most of the spray. However, with the umbrella open and placed in the bow, she stays quite dry.

An umbrella is also a handy item to have aboard on a hot, sunny day.

2 GROUND TRANSPORTATION

Bicycles

Most cruising sailors wind up walking when they get ashore—to the market, to the post office, but most importantly, to buy an ice cream cone. Few sailboats carry bicycles to get around on the beach.

We spent a couple of winters on the hook in Boot Key Harbor, Florida, and developed great leg muscles from hiking everywhere. Our neighbors, Roy and Sheila Harvey of *Aeolus*, were in the enviable position of having bikes ashore, but they hadn't carried these bikes with them. They felt the extra clutter wasn't worth the bother when they were on the move. Furthermore, as Roy remarked, "Walking sure feels good after being in the cramped quarters of a boat for several days."

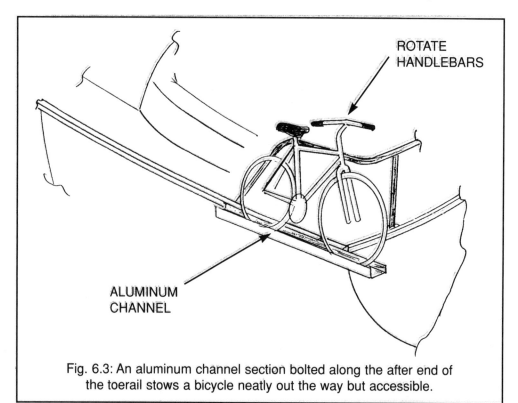

ROTATE
HANDLEBARS

ALUMINUM
CHANNEL

Fig. 6.3: An aluminum channel section bolted along the after end of the toerail stows a bicycle neatly out the way but accessible.

But once the anchors were down and Roy and Sheila settled in for a prolonged visit to a port, it was time to acquire bicycles. They searched around boatyards until they found old, trashed-out bikes, and then they refurbished them. They have even cannibalized several bikes to obtain two that were usable. But frequently, all the bikes needed were new tires, a new chain, some grease, and a can of paint, and Roy and Sheila were on their way for the entire season at minimal cost.

When the weather changed and it was time to move on, the two had a novel means of disposing of two serviceable bikes; they found a pair of needy children and made them the proud new owners of the bicycles.

You meet some fine people off cruising!

The Seagoing-Bike Rack

Carl Cathey singlehanded *Wandering Star* up to a fuel dock in Goodland, Florida. I was there to catch his docklines and admire how he stows his bicycle.

An aluminum channel section is bolted along the after end of the boat's toerail. The bolts pass through one flange, and the web of the extrusion is down.

With the bike facing aft, its wheels are set into the channel and its frame is made fast to the stern pulpit. The handlebars can be rotated out of the way. So situated, Carl's bike does not clutter the deck space, and it can be readily offloaded into the dinghy or onto a dock.

Automobiles

You've just put into Norfolk and want to get to Boston. How to do it?

Why not deliver a car? There are agencies throughout the United States that handle vehicle deliveries and are always looking for drivers. Similar contacts can often be made through newspaper want ads.

3 OPTICS

Sunglasses

Sunglasses are a must for a sailor. Primarily, they protect your eyes from the detrimental effects of sunlight. They also reduce glare and help you spot objects above or below the water's surface.

Sunglasses with polarized lenses are best for glare reduction. This is an important consideration when you try to look down into the water, since much glare is reflected off the surface. Walt Banker from the Thousands Islands of the St. Lawrence River once showed me how to verify that the lenses are truly polarized. Hold the glasses up toward the north daytime sky and rotate them as you look through a lens. If the sky grows alternately dark and light as you turn the lens, it is polarized. If there is no change in intensity, the lens is not polarized. This trick works only with north-sky light, as it is the only naturally polarized light source.

Sunglasses with yellow lenses are best for reading

water depth and spotting fish below the surface, because they filter the blue portion of the spectrum. Similarly, they are beneficial in fog, because they reduce the scattering effect of the water vapor present in the atmosphere.

Here's one last item apropos sunglasses. When one of the screws that act as a hinge on my favorite "unbreakable" sunglasses stripped out, I was desolate. Madaline snatched the glasses from me, I thought to throw them out. But no, my wonderful wife simply threaded the end of a round toothpick into the aligned holes on the bow and frame, cut the toothpick off flush, and gave the glasses back to me— an instant repair. When I asked how she learned to do this, she replied, "Women know how to do these things."

Binoculars

During the aerospace years, I was the mechanical engineer on a project team. My partner was Larry Conrad, who had spent most of his life designing lens systems. During our spare time, Larry taught me about the practical side of optics, and I told him about boats. Here are a few hints to keep in mind when purchasing a set of binoculars, courtesy of my former cohort.

The magnification power of an optical instrument is naturally important in viewing an object. But too much power can be a hindrance in hand-held binoculars or telescopes. The normal muscular twitches in a person's hands and arms make it impossible to hold anything totally still. Hence, magnification greater than seven times (7x) is not really worthwhile—you cannot see your target clearly because the image constantly jiggles. Also, as the magnification increases, the field of view, or area that you see, decreases.

The size of the objective (front) lens is very important. It determines both the size of the field of view for a given power instrument and its light-gathering capability. A pair of 7×50 binoculars has a substantially larger field of view and the image is far brighter than in a 7×35 pair. This is because the 50-millimeter lens is actually twice the size in total area. If you are interested in night vision, remember that in low-light situations, the larger the objective lens, the better the image.

When you shop for binoculars, try a pair that you like. Look at a brick wall. The lines of masonry should be straight, parallel, and sharp—on both horizontal and vertical axes. If the courses appear to bow either in or out, there is distortion in the lens system.

Next, focus on the corner of a building or the edge of a post. The line of demarcation should be sharp and distinct. Flare, a hazy edge, is an indication that color correction is not adequate, and an image cannot be focused across the full color spectrum.

Lastly, looking at a distant object, blink your eyes rapidly—right, left, right, left. The image you see by each eye should be essentially the same. If it tends to dance from side to side dramatically, the two lenses are not properly aligned.

Cameras and Film

When your camera is not in use, store it in a Ziploc plastic bag. The bag protects the equipment from the harsh marine atmosphere. If possible, place a small pack of silica gel in the bag with the camera. Silica gel is a desiccant and absorbs moisture from within the bag.

Film, both new and exposed, can be stored virtually forever in your boat's refrigerator or icebox.

4 ONBOARD TRASH COMPACTOR

The disposal of trash from cruising sailboats is becoming more and more restricted—and rightly so. There is enough plastic from our land-based civilization polluting the waters and beaches without sailors adding to this pile.

Madaline empties most food boxes and bags, such as holding cereal, sugar, and flour, into permanent containers before *Caper* ever leaves her slip. The empty boxes and wrappers go ashore immediately; removing them also minimizes the potential for a roach problem.

We keep a plastic 5-gallon bucket with a tight-fitting lid on the fantail. It is lined with a plastic bag. A plywood disk with a rope handle just fits into the pail. All our trash, including flattened cans, goes into this bucket. We mash everything in it down flat by stepping on the wooden disk. This action compacts the trash. Also the surface area is reduced, decreasing the bulk that can be readily oxidized, and the chance for odor diminishes. The filled bag is deposited ashore in a dumpster at the dinghy dock—not in someone's private refuse barrel or a business dumpster.

In a secluded anchorage, you should leave only your footprints in the sand and your vessel's wake in the water.

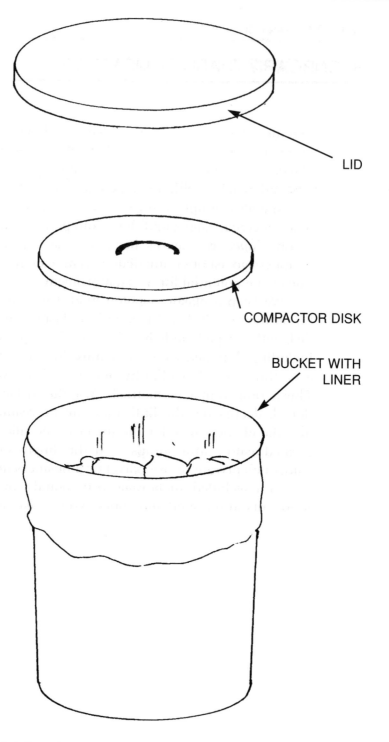

LID

COMPACTOR DISK

BUCKET WITH
LINER

Fig. 6.4: Pressing a snugly fitting wooden disk into a 5-gallon
bucket compacts refuse for easy disposal later.

VII

Odds and Ends

1 SAFETY

Quick-release Gun Rack

We try never to become involved in the ongoing discussion about whether or not to carry firearms aboard a sailboat. I grew up with guns, and Madaline is comfortable with them and can shoot. Therefore, we elect to provide ourselves afloat with the same protection that we had when we lived ashore.

The shotgun resides beside me in the forward berth. It is slung below a long shelf that runs about a foot above the bunk. A rounded teak bracket, 3 inches by 4 inches, projects down from the shelf at about the location of my knees. A hole in this bracket receives the muzzle end of the

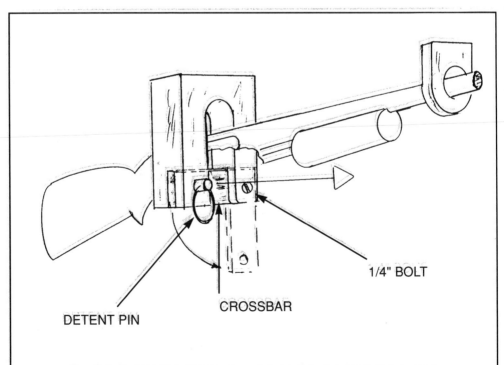

1/4" BOLT

CROSSBAR

DETENT PIN

Fig. 7.1: Pulling the detent pin releases the gun from this custom rack mounted under a shelf alongside the forward berth.

weapon. Near my elbow is a second bracket, this one shaped like the inverted letter U. Its legs are slotted to accommodate a plastic crossbar 1/4 inch thick by 1/2 inch high. This bar is secured in the leg nearest the hull by a 1/4-inch bolt that acts as a pivot. The other end of the plastic bar is locked into the opposite leg by a quick-release detent pin with a ring through one end. The gun's action rests on the plastic crossbar. Tugging the pin releases the crossbar, allowing the shotgun to fall free.

Incidentally, we have never had occasion even to consider using the gun.

Actuating an Alarm System

One gray dreary day up north, I lay loafing on the settee. Madaline returned from a visit down the basin and stepped aboard. I felt the boat's distinctive slight roll, but also heard a squeak. Poking around, I found that *Caper's* side deck bore ever so slightly against a nonstructural locker bulkhead—the source of the noise. It occurred to me that a boat's decks must flex under load and that this slight movement could be put to use to trigger an alarm system.

Using a dial indicator, I found that the deck did indeed deflect about 0.005 inch under my wife's footstep. By using a multiplying linkage, I was able to actuate a microswitch to energize an alarm. The linkage is a simple lever that can

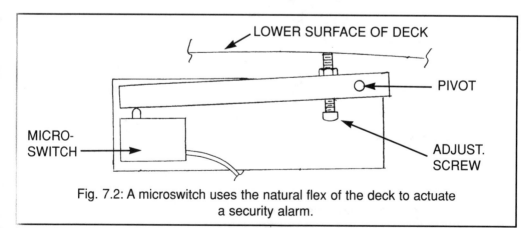

Fig. 7.2: A microswitch uses the natural flex of the deck to actuate a security alarm.

be run out to bear against the underside of the deck. An adjustable screw is set 1 inch from the pivot. The contact of the microswitch is positioned 3 inches from the pivot. This setup provides a 3:1 ratio of motion—enough to close the switch. One such mechanism is secured beneath the deck, midway between the toerail and the edge of the cabin, on each side of the boat.

We seldom use the alarm system, but it's comforting to know that it is there to use if we so choose. In some areas, it is good to be able to announce loudly that an intruder has just come aboard your boat—a shrieking siren or Klaxon horn does just that.

Protecting Your Valuables

Folks who live ashore have access to safety deposit boxes and safes to protect their valuables. Full-time cruisers and most liveaboards do not have this luxury and must devise other options.

We have aboard a lockable, watertight steel box about the size and shape of an attaché case. In it we keep such items as insurance documents, passports, *Caper*'s title, and other personal objects. It is stowed beneath our big forward berth. In an emergency, it is easy to grab the box and run—hurricane Andrew in 1992 proved that.

John D. MacDonald's fictional adventurer Travis McGee often spoke of the hidey-hole built into his *Busted Flush*. We have one, too. It's not very large, but darned hard to find. Off cruising, we pack our cruising kitty cash into a plastic container that once held a new roll of electrical tape. It is watertight and fits nicely into the hidey-hole. Determined thieves might eventually find the money, but looking for it would surely slow them down. If you are ever searched by customs or Coast Guard officials, it might be

wise to mention the existence of a secret hiding place before hand.

Snorkeling

Many people choke while they are snorkeling when they in-
gest seawater through the breathing tube. Chuck Miller, my
scuba instructor, explained how to prevent this unpleasant
experience.

Place the tip of your tongue against the roof of your
mouth. The tongue acts as a check valve, and your gag re-
flex prevents you from ingesting water.

Surf Swimming

We sailors swim beside our boats in lakes and rivers, in
tidal lagoons, and even in the ocean on those calm days of
long, easy swells. And nearly all of us are drawn to the
seashore. Bobbing in the surf, swimming, riding the crash-
ing waves, or just walking at the water's edge—and eventually getting wet—is a wonderful form of relaxation. Most of
us who sail are moderately strong swimmers and feel con-
fident of our abilities.

But think again. Surf swimming is not a pastime to be
taken casually. It demands some of the same caution that
we exercise when we're aboard a sailing vessel nearing
land. Tides and currents exist along the shore that can be
life threatening. Understanding these forces and knowing
how to deal with them can prevent an enjoyable afternoon
from turning into a tragedy.

Although the exact contour of the ocean floor near a
given beach front is constantly changing, shorelines follow
a general configuration. The beach slopes downward from
barrier sand dunes to the point where it is lost beneath the

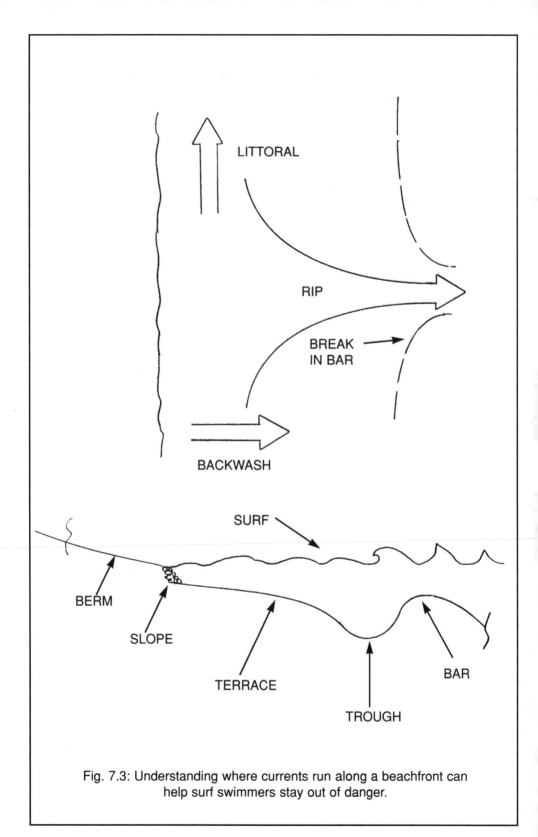

Fig. 7.3: Understanding where currents run along a beachfront can help surf swimmers stay out of danger.

waves. Technically, this incline is referred to as the berm. The place where the waves break and tumble is the beach face. It is composed of disintegrating shell or rounded stones and often becomes steep. Out beyond the face lies a somewhat more placid stretch of flat sandy bottom that is appropriately called the terrace. The terrace gradually gives way to a trough parallel to the shore that is often 6 to 10 feet deep at low tide. A sandbar forms about 100 yards offshore. The bar acts as a brake to the ocean waves, forcing them upward and slowing them. The wave crests become unstable and tumble forward, becoming breakers. Here is where surfers pick up their rides.

As soon as a wave crashes upon the beach, the water loses its energy and recedes, making room for the next surge. The rushing water being drawn back to sea sometimes erodes the sandbar to form a canyonlike channel. Water funneling rapidly through this tidal cut can sweep even able swimmers far out beyond the beach. It is virtually impossible to make any headway swimming against this rip current. But you can escape by swimming across the stream—in line with shore—until you are free of the dangerous rip.

A surf swimmer may encounter two other currents that are less dangerous. Backwashes occur along steeply sloping beach faces, also creating a strong offshore flow of water. This occurs much closer to shore, however, and incoming waves generally counteract the force of this backwash current. A swimmer can usually ride a backwash out by simply floating until the stream ceases. Strong swimmers can also overcome the flow by swimming straight for shore.

Littoral currents sweep along parallel to the shoreline. You can detect their presence when you spot waves breaking at an angle with the beach. Swimmers can escape their tug by also swimming toward the shore at an angle, going slightly with the current.

No one should go swimming when heavy seas are running. Severe injuries can be inflicted from tumbling in the surf and being slammed head-first against the sea bottom. And if surfers are in the area, avoid them. Surfboard fins can produce severe cuts on swimmers caught in their paths.

Another pleasant pastime along the beach is simply flopping on an inflatable raft and drifting peacefully along. There is little risk as long as a sea breeze is blowing. But extreme caution should be taken if the wind is off the land. You can be quickly swept far out from shore. If you find yourself in this situation and have any doubts about your ability to swim back to shore, stay with the raft. It will increase your visibility and make your rescue much easier.

After a day of sailing, with the boat lying to anchor behind a barrier island, nothing is better than an exhilarating swim in the surf—if you heed these few precautions.

2 SEAFOOD

Boiling Shrimp

Good fresh shrimp must be cooked properly. And most folk don't know how.

Our method may not be elegant, but it works for us. Here's how we prepare shrimp aboard *Caper:* Bring the water to a boil, and when it is rolling, add the shrimp and a handful of celery leaves. The leaves flavor the shrimp slightly. More importantly, they absorb the cooking odor, which can be overpowering in the close quarters of a boat.

As soon as the water boils again, the shrimps are pink and ready to devour. Remove them immediately, since over-cooking makes them doughy.

If possible, buy your shrimps with the heads on—they are less expensive that way. But also we're told by fishermen that there is a pouch of fat in the shrimp's head that adds to the flavor. Remove the heads after you boil the shrimp; the body is then easy to devein.

Cleaning Fish

Guess I'll never make it as a fisherman; I'm too much a sailor. Even so, I was captain for Dr. Bruce Miller aboard *Doc's Toy* for several months. Doc claimed that the boat from the helm forward was his wife's motor yacht, but from the wheel aft she was his fishing boat. And he tried hard to make a fisherman out of me—the poor misguided soul.

Every now and then, I trail a line over the stern when *Caper* is sailing. And sometimes I land our supper. Then two tricks Doc taught me come to mind, and I use them.

Returning from the fishing grounds, Doc and I filled a bucket with clean seawater. As grouper fillets and tuna steaks came off the cleaning table, we rinsed them in this seawater. No freshwater rinse for Doc. He maintained that the chemicals in tap water taint and mask the true taste of the fish. I must say that I agree with him.

Now for the gruesome part. After the flesh was re-moved, the remains of the fish were tossed into the water as food for crabs, lobster, and the like. But before Doc dis-carded the carcass, he insisted that the stomach and eye-balls be punctured. This simple act prevents gas from pocketing in these organs and floating the decaying body to the surface. Look at many charterboat docks the morning after—it can be a grizzly sight. Too bad more folk don't take a moment to pierce the carcass the way Doc Miller does.

Glass-bottom Buckets

Many boats are equipped with glass-bottom buckets for underwater viewing and spotting fish. If you cut a plywood insert to nest into the bottom of the bucket, it will protect the clear plastic window from abrasion. And then you can tote things in it on snorkel and diving expeditions.

Our glass-bottom bucket is actually a piece of large-diameter, heavy-wall plastic pipe. This configuration can be made longer to make viewing from a dinghy easier. It also weighs more and is less buoyant, so the viewing window stays beneath the surface of the water more readily.

3 HOLIDAYS: THE GIFT LIST

Last spring, your parents shocked the entire family. Just after Dad's retirement, they sold the house, moved aboard their sailboat, and went off cruising. Now, in October, they have written to say that they plan to leave the boat for a few weeks in Pascagoula, Spanish Wells, or some other strange-sounding place and will be spending Christmas with you.

"Wonderful," you think, "what a great reunion!" But then you try to imagine what sort of gifts you can give people who wander all over while living on a 35-foot boat.

We are some of those people who have run away to sea, so perhaps we can offer a few hints.

Bear in mind that the folks no longer have any appreciable storage space, so many unnecessary items won't really be welcome. If it's fragile, prone to rust or mildew, or consumes electrical power—forget it.

By now, they will have learned that anything other than 100 percent cotton is simply too hot in the lower latitudes. So except for a special sweater for cold days, avoid synthetics. Naturally, farther north, woolens will be most welcome. We like T-shirts, particularly those with some whimsical decoration such as "Surf Ohio" or "Sail Wyoming" or those celebrating the Port Huron to Mackinac Race, since the former is Madaline's hometown. Shirts, sweaters, and windbreakers can be given a special touch by embroidering the boat's name on them.

Photographs are always welcome, but remember, space is limited, so make them wallet sized. Most cruising boats have a prominent place for family pictures, usually grouped in a collage. Pictures of family, particularly children, are constantly going out of date, so they are one gift that can be repeated year after year.

The library is now a catch-all term. Most sailors are avid readers. Aboard *Caper*, paperback books are always welcome. Some books we'll save to read again, but others will be traded off to replenish our supply. It's wise to know if your recipients have favorite authors, but any bestseller will probably be appreciated. Practical boating books will also be of use.

Most boats have stereo systems, and a new tape or CD by some favorite artist makes a nice gift. Instructional language tapes are also appreciated if the boat is headed for foreign ports.

Small personal radios and cassette players equipped with headsets that can be worn while working on the brightwork, standing watch alone, or sunning on the foredeck make good gifts, but don't forget to include a supply of AA batteries. Packages of flashlight batteries, both C and D cell size, are also welcome. Speaking of flashlights, how about one or two of the miniature lights with the high-intensity lamps? No boat can be overstocked with these.

Some sailboats are now equipped with a VCR, which opens up a whole new area of gift possibilities: recent release movies, family events, tutorials, cruising guides—the list goes on.

Special gifts make the holidays for cruising sailors. A son bakes a fruitcake following the old family recipe, one daughter sends exotic blends of coffee, another forwards fine chocolate, a friend provides butter-rich and rum-soaked cakes, and another box arrives filled with Christmas cookies. Then when yachties gather in a secluded anchorage for "orphan's Christmas," everyone has some goodies to share and sweet memories to savor. Obviously, gifts of this nature must be selected for their ability to travel well in addition to their taste.

We received one such care package in its own canvas boat bag. The treats are long gone, but the bag has seen many a trip ashore to haul groceries and supplies back aboard.

Perhaps Dad has a taste for good scotch or bourbon and Mom likes an occasional glass of fine wine. A carefully thought out liquor locker can be an excellent gift for the holidays afloat as well as ashore.

All cruising sailors look forward to getting mail at the next port. Even if they usually are not letter writers, they develop the habit so that friends and relatives will respond. As a result, note paper, stationery bearing the boat name, and similar items make choice presents. One of the most thoughtful and original gifts one recent Christmas came from a daughter who supplied us with several books of postage stamps.

Another possibility is to provide airfare for a visit by

your cruising sailors. Most of us out cruising are on limited budgets, so travel—especially at holiday time—can be a financial drain. This gift need not be an expensive one; the son of one couple we know has a job that requires him to fly extensively on commercial airlines. Thus, he manages to supply his parents with frequent flyer passes.

When all else fails, give your cruising family a gift certificate to one of the large mail-order houses for marine supplies, clothing, or foodstuffs. Or simply ask the folks what they would really like for a gift. Deep down, Mom probably wants a new stove and Dad a new outboard for the dinghy, but they will surely have more reasonably priced items in mind for suggestions.

Here is a short list of possible stocking stuffers to consider: a bag of wire ties, one pound of assorted stainless steel screws, an assortment of crimp fittings for wire splices, and airtight plastic food containers.

One last item remains. The folks will probably arrive carrying a few pounds of the finest shrimp that you have ever eaten as a contribution to the holiday table. After the gifts have been opened and the dinner cleared away, be sure to sit back and listen—for, oh the stories they will tell!

This material first appeared in *Great Lakes Sailor*, November 1991.